A FEAST OF WORDS

Also by Anna Shapiro

Christmas 1996

Merry Christmas Mom!
Thank you for the many literary and culinary feasts you have shared with us.

Love,
Andy, Chris, Ben & Alex

A FEAST of WORDS

for Lovers

of Food and Fiction

ANNA SHAPIRO

with drawings by the author

W · W · NORTON & COMPANY

New York   London

The text of this book is composed in 11/13 Fairfield LH Light

with the display set in Fairfield LH Medium and Light

Composition and manufacturing by The Haddon Craftsmen Inc.

Book design by Margaret M. Wagner

Library of Congress Cataloging-in-Publication Data

Shapiro, Anna.

A feast of words : for lovers of food and fiction / by Anna Shapiro.

p. cm.

Includes bibliographical references and index.

ISBN 0-393-03979-X

1. Food in literature.   2. Cookery in literature.   3. Food

-Fiction.   I. Title.

PN56.F59S52   1996

809.3'9355—dc20   96-2514

CIP

W. W. Norton & Company, Inc., 500 Fifth Avenue, New York, N.Y. 10110

http://web.wwnorton.com

W. W. Norton & Company Ltd., 10 Coptic Street, London WC1A 1PU

1 2 3 4 5 6 7 8 9 0

To my wonderful father, David Shapiro, who read me my first
books, and who often cooked for all of us.

and

In loving memory of Laurie Colwin, who fed me when I was
hungry; whose inspiring writing about food I was lucky to
illustrate; and, most of all, whose witty definitiveness I relished
in conversation.

if you can get nothing better out of the world,
get a good dinner out of it, at least.

—HERMAN MELVILLE
Moby-Dick

CONTENTS

PENITENTIAL MEALS

FOOD OF LOVE

BREAD OF AFFLICTION

STARVED LOVE

EATING THE SOCIAL INDEX

THE COOK DID IT, or KILLING WITH KINDNESS

TIME ITSELF

Recipes

APPETIZERS

MEAT AND POULTRY

FISH

CONDIMENTS

DESSERTS

BEVERAGES

FOREWORD

Literature is nourishment. It is brain food, food for character, mood-altering. It feeds the starved soul as well as the merely bored one. It is the nitrogen that makes the imagination bloom, it opens the runnel of hope to thirsty desperation. If you are happy, healthy, settled in mind, a novel is the luxury of mere amusement. But who is in such a state always, or even often? As you wait for the judge's verdict on custody arrangements, for chemotherapy to work, to start liking people at your new job, that same book, that former luxury, may become sustenance. Moral sustenance, to be sure: sustaining you to eat your bread of affliction, as in *A Little Princess,* where it is the heroine's ability to project herself into the fiction of being royalty that keeps her going through neglect and abuse.

A Feast of Words was inspired by novels that have fed me and thousands of others. It is about food—with recipes and menus—and about how food is used to tell stories. In a work of fiction, elaborate exposition may be required for a reader to believe why, say, a man hates himself, but little is required for the plausibility of his hatred of cooked beef liver. What is common to the novels and stories highlighted in this volume is that they use the liver to show a man's state of mind. The food scenes excerpted here are rarely scenes of sumptuousness and excess. This is not a book about gluttony. Though food may be present to supply atmosphere or background or verisimilitude in these stories, it doesn't only do those things: without the food, the story in question would be broken-backed, useless, with a critical link in the plot or key to character missing. If there were no dinner scene in *Alice Adams,* Alice would get the guy. If there were no joint of meat in "Lamb to the Slaughter," that philandering husband would be living happily with his new love. Without the crucial item of food, Jane Somers, in *The Diary of a Good Neighbour,* might never discover what it is to love; Rose in "Royal Beatings" might successfully be able to resist her stepmother and escape despising herself; Ethan Frome might have found some way to be with his Mattie. We would have eternal summer if Persephone hadn't eaten that pomegranate.

Again and again, as I went back into my chosen works of fiction to seek out their passages about food, I was astonished to discover how very central food was to the books, even though I'd chosen them for that reason. I knew that part of the cure for tuberculosis in *The Magic Mountain* was overfeeding, but I did not remember that hermetically preserved food was the central metaphor in a book as overabundant in contradictory meanings as the Berghof tables are in redundant dishes. I had read Levin's luncheon scene with Oblonsky in *Anna Karenina* I don't know how many times without seeing that it contained, in its relatively trim confines, the whole fat book. I remembered the exquisite meals Leonora Eyre cooked for her two beaux in *The Sweet Dove Died*, but had not noticed that the entire progress of the story is represented in those meals. Some of the entries in this collection are little more than dramatized recipes, like James Cain's for iguana stew—a recipe that has you on the edge of your seat.

More prosaically, if less prosily, people who create with words often find relief from that medium in the more certain formulations of the kitchen—a soufflé is so much more likely to turn out than a short story, and takes less time. Barbara Pym liked to relax with cookbooks, and everybody likes to eat. In reading and eating, "taste" resolves its ambiguity and finds its common meaning: based purely on anecdotal evidence, I've observed that the incidence of appreciative eaters among passionate readers runs especially high. Since the recipes here are for readers, I haven't worried about being literal— the dishes are often metaphorical matches to the food in the stories: I didn't think there would be great call for frumenty (*The Mayor of Casterbridge*) or burnt porridge (*Jane Eyre*). It's hard to get iguana at the butcher's.

For the most part, I've stuck to recipes I've used and honed for years, collected in a little looseleaf notebook whose pages are covered with scrawled annotations. For some of the grander or more exotic dishes, like those for a version of Babette's opulent feast, I researched a variety of cookbooks, experimented in my kitchen, and tried to come up with what was comfortably and reasonably cookable by the home cook. Some people hate to share their cooking "secrets"; I like my guests to groan with pleasure and go home stuffed, and I want yours to, likewise. I don't want the cook to groan in agony. I am not a chef, and I don't expect my readers to be trained at the Cordon Bleu.

The steps in the recipes are organized for ease and clarity, so that you aren't asked, halfway through cooking something, to add broth you didn't know you needed to make. But if a cookbook is a kind of textbook, mine is a textbook for a progressive school: I hope readers will take these recipes not as didactic formulas to be rigidly followed, but as guidelines that their own tastes and experiences will lead them to expand and adjust. You should never feel you *must* use a wire whisk to make a salad dressing, or that if you don't have a food processor or food mill, you are sunk. Also, it seems to me that, if there is anything in common between writing fiction and cooking food, it is the ability to imagine how certain qualities will combine. Everyone has the talent to some degree: even making a peanut butter and jelly sandwich, you know whether it tastes better to you with raspberry jam or grape jelly; on chewy pumpernickel or white toast. When you have tried and learned and tasted from a recipe, that is when you can begin to make it truly your own.

Because this is a book to read as well as cook from, its organization follows the logic of the fictional works discussed. The entries are categorized by the role food plays in the stories. Food is so rich and potent in its value as metaphor, however, that many of the works could fit in several categories. Affliction of one kind or another is far from figuring only in the books gathered under "Bread of Affliction," a characterization that could suit *Jane Eyre* almost as well as *A Little Princess* and *Moby-Dick.* It is depressing how many works by women could fall into "Penitential Meals." The most populous category features food as anything but life-giving: food kills people in "The Cook Did It."

Less accountable (to me) is why so many of the titles in this collection are proper names: Emma, Anna Karenina, Bontshe Shvayg, Julie de Carneilhan, David Copperfield, Moby Dick, Ethan Frome, Jane Eyre, Alice Adams, Marjorie Morningstar.

One thing this collection is not: compendious. It isn't scholarly either. I write novels, and the descriptions of the stories constitute a novelist's view. For readers who have not gotten around to seemingly formidable tomes like *Remembrance of Things Past* or *The Magic Mountain,* I hope what I've written will convey a lively sense of such works in all their delight, if not their full scope.

For me the selections make a kind of covert autobiography. I spent so much of my youth reading these books that it seems to have lasted for the entire nineteenth century and half the twentieth. The recipes too are markers on a private emotional map. "Chicken Livers in White Wine" conjures a rooming house in Toronto where I first cooked it, on a hot plate. I think of the commune in Ithaca where granola was repeatedly drawn from the oven for stirring one very hot day. And any number of the dishes bring back a tiny New York apartment where big, ambitious meals were served to people I loved.

—*Anna Shapiro*

MORAL FIBER

EMMA

by Jane Austen

(1 8 1 6)

Most readers of Jane Austen would not think of her as a great dweller upon food; she is known as a great dweller upon character. Where she does mention food, it is then no great surprise that it is there not for tone or mood or background but as a means of pointing with almost excruciating exactitude to qualities of character among those serving, eating, gathering, or talking about it. In *Emma,* there are two scenes devolving upon food: one, a minor dinner (in terms of consequence) early in the book, and another, much more important one later on as various plots have come or are coming, not coincidentally, to fruition.

Emma Woodhouse is allowed to be at her best in the early dinner scene, both practical and diplomatic, a rare moment in this book when the heroine is not being punished to some degree for thinking just a little too well of her own powers of observation and persuasion. Here those abilities serve her perfectly, and her fussy father's contradictory but self-involved niceties make an ideal foil for them as she tries to ensure that their guests won't have to suffer the privations her father believes best for their health. As it happens, Mr. Woodhouse is correct in believing cereal to be healthier than the fancy dishes Emma puts forward. But the Woodhouses' guests are not well off, certainly getting enough of porridge in their ordinary lives, and Emma has all the proper instincts of a hostess in insisting on a rich and festive meal:

> With an alacrity beyond the common impulse of a spirit which yet was never indifferent to the credit of doing everything well and attentively, with the real good-will of a mind delighted with its own ideas, did she then do all the honours of the meal, and help and recommend the minced

chicken and scalloped oysters, with an urgency which she knew would be acceptable to the early hours and civil scruples of their guests.

Upon such occasions poor Mr. Woodhouse's feelings were in sad warfare. He loved to have the cloth laid, because it had been the fashion of his youth, but his conviction of suppers being very unwholesome made him rather sorry to see anything put on it; and while his hospitality would have welcomed his visitors to everything, his care for their health made him grieve that they would eat.

Such another small basin of thin gruel as his own was all that he could, with thorough self-approbation, recommend; though he might constrain himself, while the ladies were comfortably clearing the nicer things, to say—

"Mrs. Bates, let me propose your venturing on one of these eggs. An egg boiled very soft is not unwholesome. Serle understands boiling an egg better than anybody. I would not recommend an egg boiled by anybody else—but you need not be afraid, they are very small, you see—one of our small eggs will not hurt you. Miss Bates, let Emma help you to a *little* bit of tart—a *very* little bit. Ours are all apple-tarts. You need not be afraid of unwholesome preserves here. I do not advise the custard. Mrs. Goddard, what say you to *half* a glass of wine? A *small* half-glass, put into a tumbler of water? I do not think it could disagree with you."

Emma allowed her father to talk—but supplied her visitors in a much more satisfactory style; and on the present evening had particular pleasure in sending them away happy.

There are no real villains in Jane Austen's novels, but the interfering married ladies who crop up again and again in them, though appearing as comic characters, really are, within the terms of these fictional worlds, very close to being evil. Such a one is Mrs. Elton, a social upstart with no sense of the grossness of her presumption. She calls the first gentleman of the district, known even to his oldest friends as "mister," merely "Knightley," invites not only herself but a whole party to his estate, Donwell, and there reveals herself to be, on top of her other shortcomings, a solid hypocrite.

It all comes about because Mr. Knightley makes the mistake of teasing her by saying, "Come and eat my strawberries; they are ripening fast."

If Mr. Knightley did not begin seriously, he was obliged to proceed so; for his proposal was caught at with delight; and the "Oh! I should like it of all things," was not plainer in words than manner. Donwell was famous for its strawberry-beds, which seemed a plea for the invitation; but no plea was necessary; cabbage-beds would have been enough to tempt the lady . . . "It is to be a morning scheme, you know, Knightley; quite a simple thing. I shall wear a large bonnet, and bring one of my little baskets hanging on my arm. Here—probably this basket with pink ribbon . . ."

Politeness dictates that Mr. Knightley not refuse, so the event takes place. If you knew nothing else about Mrs. Elton, you would know everything you needed to from the passage in which she gathers the fruit of her scheme. It is a tour de force, an entire character and scene compressed in a single paragraph.

Mrs. Elton, in all her apparatus of happiness, her large bonnet and her basket, was very ready to lead the way in gathering, accepting, or talking. Strawberries, and only strawberries, could now be thought or spoken of. "The best fruit in England—everybody's favourite—always wholesome. These the finest beds and finest sorts. Delightful to gather for one's self—the only way of really enjoying them. Morning decidedly the best time—never tired—every sort good—hautboy infinitely superior—no comparison—the others hardly eatable—hautboys very scarce—Chili preferred—white wood finest flavour of all—price of strawberries in London—abundance about Bristol—Maple Grove—cultivations—beds when to be renewed—gardeners thinking exactly different—no general rule—gardeners never to be put out of their way—delicious fruit—only too rich to be eaten much of—inferior to cherries—currants more refreshing—only objections to gathering strawberries the stooping—glaring sun—tired to death—could bear it no longer—must go and sit in the shade."

It is on this fruit-gathering expedition that Emma's eyes are at last opened. She sees Donwell as if for the first time, and in Austen, to appreciate the household establishment is to love the man: it begins to dawn on Emma that she has been behaving ridiculously not only in regard to everyone else's love life (which has constituted her major occupation throughout the book), but in relation to her own. As a result of this excursion, she comes to see herself as having been no less despicable and self-flattering than Mrs. Elton.

Done well, indeed.

For centuries in Europe, fruit was regarded as no more than a laxative or, at best, a condiment. So strawberries, if picked at all, were picked wild. Then, in the sixteenth century, strawberries became a fad in England. It became a kind of hobby—or craze—in the "great houses" to cultivate them, which meant that strawberries to buy were expensive, and a real symbol of wealth. Hautboys—also called "hotboys"—were difficult to garden, and the most popular variety. It seems significant that the pre-eminent hybridizer of the early nineteenth century, when *Emma* was written, was named Knight, and his hybrids famously the "Elton seedling" and "Elton pine." It is possible that for Austen's knowledgeable contemporaries, the strawberry scene's crucial place in the drama would have been telegraphed long since by the characters' names, and would constitute a little extratextual joke.

O n the whole, the large-size, commercially cultivated late-twentieth-century strawberries available in markets are not worth eating, much less paying for. Though you can get strawberries all year round in that form, the sweetest and most intensely strawberry-ish berries are the ones that can't be shipped and so are locally grown, in season. Even the bloated hybrids are delicious this way. But the sweetest and most delicate flavors are in the small field strawberries that can sometimes be picked wild—they have a bright, sharp taste—or bought at a farmers' market. Some of the cultivated field species are "day neutral," which means they continue to grow and be harvested through all the warmer months.

There are, as everyone knows, a plethora of desserts using strawberries, from strawberry shortcake to strawberry-rhubarb pie. But if the berries are good, it seems a shame to cook or bury them. They are delicious sprinkled with confectioners' sugar or cocoa, with butter cookies and vanilla ice cream on the side. Julienned mint leaves will do no harm.

An elegant treatment of large June strawberries is to dip them in liquid chocolate. If you really want to paint the lily, you can set out whipped cream and let your guests dip their chocolate-coated strawberries in that.

Chocolate-Dipped Strawberries

8 ounces or more semisweet baker's chocolate
Ripe strawberries

1. Melt the chocolate over fully bubbling water in a double boiler. Remove from heat.
2. Holding them by the stem, dip the strawberries one by one, leaving the upper half red. Place on waxed paper to harden. (Refrigeration will hasten the process.)
3. Serve with any or all the accompaniments mentioned in text above, at room temperature or only slightly cooler. Dipped berries may also be used to decorate a whipped-cream-coated cake.

This dessert could accompany a late-morning snack such as is enjoyed at Knightley's, or a light summer lunch of chilled dishes:

LIGHT SUMMER LUNCH

Rice and chick-pea salad with parsley, scallions, red sweet peppers, mayonnaise, and dash of horseradish

Fish Shape (recipe follows)

Sliced cucumbers with sweetened Vinaigrette*

Chocolate-Dipped Strawberries (recipe above)

Coffee iced with coffee cubes

*Recipe in *The Sweet Dove Died*.

Fish Shape

1 6-ounce can salmon or tuna or equivalent amount fresh
1 cup heavy (not ultrapasteurized) cream or evaporated milk,
   or 1 cup whole milk plus 1 tablespoon butter
1 cup bread crumbs
Salt and pepper
2 eggs, well beaten

Preheat oven to 350°.

1. If using canned salmon, remove skin and bones. Mash fish.
2. Heat cream or, if using milk, melt the butter in it. Remove from heat and add all the other ingredients when cool enough so eggs won't be prematurely cooked.
3. Grease a 1-quart fish mold well. Pour in fish mixture. Place the mold in a pan of hot water and bake 1 hour.
4. Unmold immediately to serve hot, or cool and chill before unmolding to serve cold. Fish shape can be served either plain or with white sauce if hot, or with home-made mayonnaise if cold.

Serves 4 to 5.

ANNA KARENINA
by Leo Tolstoy
(1 8 7 7)

Some of Chapter 9, and all of chapters 10 and 11 in Part I of *Anna Karenina* concern a meal—lunch. The meal is as enormous as the space devoted to it, but not a disproportionate number of pages in relation to the length of the book (807 pages in a paperback edition with narrow margins and small print). Still, it is of minor consequence in terms of the large actions of the plot: Levin (a character at least as central as Anna, despite the title) is thinking about proposing to a woman about half his age, Kitty, who is the youngest sister to the wife of the man who is his lunch companion, Oblonsky. Oblonsky encourages Levin's romantic hopes; he himself has just been caught cheating on his wife, and she has nearly left him. The two old friends really are talking at cross-purposes throughout this gargantuan meal, each preoccupied with his own very different love troubles. But everything throughout the meal, and about it, expresses their antagonistic attitudes to love, women, marriage, and the purpose of life. Really, the whole of this enormous book is contained in the meanings of this passage; in the language, more or less, of food.

Levin, visiting from his country estate, has just been skating with his beloved on a Moscow pond, and is ravenous. Still, when Oblonsky proposes turbot (at the restaurant he has chosen because he owes more there "and therefore considered it wrong to avoid it"), Levin has agreed only absently, because he is thinking solely of Oblonsky's young sister-in-law Kitty. (Levin's response, "Oh yes, I'm *awfully* fond of turbot," makes you smile because you know he's really saying, "I'm awfully fond of *Kitty*"; he doesn't know what he's saying, but it's certainly not about turbot.) So Levin doesn't care if Oblonsky changes his mind at the waiter's suggestion and orders oysters (three dozen for the two of them, following vodka "with a bit of fish"), and then soup, the turbot after all (with "sauce Beaumarchais"), roast beef, then capon, and a fruit macedoine for dessert, with Parmesan taken between courses—plus a bottle of champagne and two others of "classic" Chablis.

To a twentieth-century American reader, it seems like a truly disgusting amount of food, and if most readers ponder this scene at all, it is to remember the magnitude of the meal, with its two or three sets of appetizers and three main courses. What is odd is that Tolstoy meant you to think it disgusting too, in that such a meal represented an indecent norm in imperial Russia among aristocrats and landowners. In reviewing an English translation of *Classic Russian Cooking,* the pre-eminent pre-Revolutionary household guide, Tatiana Tolstaia (a distant descendant of the great Count Leo) refers to "the fabulous bacchanalia of gluttony that raged on those yellowing pages," and to this "lost era of culinary titans, maniacs with cast-iron intestines as long as fire hoses, with stomachs of elephantine proportions, with the jaws of ancient Charybdis, who devoured entire ships and their oarsmen at one sitting," in relation to whom "one feels oneself a pathetic, feeble dwarf." She goes on to relate this grotesque diet to the eventual Bolshevik revolution: while the servants prepare these titanic meals, their own *holiday* food is no more than a soup of boiled beef tripe, potatoes, and "second-rate" flour, "No greens, no spices, no joy."

Amid the too-many courses, Levin says he would rather be eating cabbage soup or buckwheat porridge. (When the waiter overhears this, Tolstoy cruelly satirizes the strained gentility always exemplified for him in his class's use of French by having him inquire, "Porridge *à la Russe,* sir?" about this dish that represents the absolute of unpretension.) As he tucks into his oysters, Levin is aware that he would rather be eating "white bread and cheese." (One is surprised that the bread would be white, not the healthier dark peasant bread.) They get to the crux of the matter before even reaching the soup. "You don't care much for oysters, do you?" says Oblonsky. Levin remarks that

> "I can't help regarding it as strange that while we in the country try to get our meals over as quickly as possible so as to be able to get on with our work, you and I are doing our best to make our dinner last as long as possible and for that reason have oysters."
>
> "Well, naturally," Oblonsky put in. "But that's the whole aim of civilization: to make everything a source of enjoyment."
>
> "Well, if that is so, I'd rather be a savage."

Oblonsky, never looking past sensual and social pleasure, advises Levin to go ahead and propose to Kitty, since, even if she refuses him, "every girl is proud of a proposal of marriage." As Levin has suspected, however, with-

out being able to tell exactly what is going on, Kitty's mother has been encouraging the girl to turn down the bread-and-cheese of Levin and go for the
roast beef, champagne, and oysters of Count Vronsky. Oblonsky doesn't
know this either. He tells Levin that his spouse, Kitty's sister, "says that Kitty
is sure to be your wife." She is right, but none of them knows what pain all
the protagonists will have suffered by the time that happy goal can be
achieved.

After considering Levin's prospects with Kitty, Oblonsky obliquely alludes
to his own troubles, following the turbot and going on to the second bottle
of Chablis:

> "Suppose you're married and you love your wife, but you've fallen in love
> with another woman . . ."
>
> "I'm sorry, but I really can't understand that. I mean it's . . . just as
> incomprehensible to me as if, after having eaten a good dinner now, I
> were to go into a baker's shop and steal a roll."
>
> Oblonsky's eyes sparkled more than usual.
>
> "Why not? Rolls sometimes smell so good that you can't resist them!"

Even Levin smiles at this, but when Oblonsky, growing uncharacteristi-
cally gloomy, claims to be lost and asks "What's to be done?" Levin still
replies, "Don't steal rolls." That's the story of the whole book, really (minus
everything that makes it wonderful, a world map of the human heart): don't
lust after sauce Beaumarchais, don't steal rolls. Anna steals the roll that is
Vronsky and finds life an eternal punishment; Kitty, also having chosen that
good-looking capon Vronsky (you could say he's the opposite, but in Tolstoyan
terms he isn't really manly), is humiliated and also nearly dies of self-reproach;
Oblonsky gets away with stealing his rolls (and having them too), but his
cheerful wrongdoing is not sanctioned.

While Tolstoy was horrified by "looseness" in women (he has Levin com-
paring the feeling to Oblonsky's abhorrence of spiders), he was pretty horrified by looseness in himself. He was such a creature of lust that he casually
grabbed a peasant from the side of the road and raped her, and used un-
countable others as well—but never after he was married. (When he reached
a certain age, he castigated himself for wanting sex even with his wife, but
continued to desire her—and also to hate her—into his eighties.) In some
sense he accepted that what was sauce for the goose was sauce for the gan-
der: that *neither* should have sauce. Or steal rolls.

A n d that is why I am offering not a recipe for oysters (according to the American Littoral Society, no shellfish on the Eastern seaboard is uncontaminated) or even turbot (the same environmental group counsels against frequent eating of fish altogether), much less beef or capon. You are getting cabbage soup. (More or less: borscht has cabbage in it.) The beef in it is optional. It is, either way, full of greens, spices, and joy.

Tolstoy eventually became a vegetarian. In environmental terms, eating meat is no plus—a resource-wasting luxury. That is why the wealthy classes ate so much of it. Ordinary people, not just in those days but in much of the world today, have been lucky to get any kind of protein every few days—or weeks or months. A middle-class American has the luxury of making the issue a moral choice. In that respect I have gone by this standard: if you would be willing to kill it yourself, by all means feel free to eat it. I once ate—without entirely knowing I was doing so in time, I must concede—a chicken I had raised. The little downy thing had slept in my room at night, and in my cupped hands after it woke, screeching, at dawn until my rising time every morning. It cooked up gristley. I'm afraid I think the following soup is much, much better with meat.

Borscht

for the soup base

> 1 pound brisket (optional)
> 1 pound meaty shinbone (optional)
> 2 quarts water, or 1 quart water and
>   1 quart beef broth
> 1 teaspoon salt (optional)
> 2 thick slices bacon
> 1 large onion, chopped
> 2 stalks celery, chopped
> 1 large beet, grated
> 2 cloves garlic, cut in half
> 2 cups fresh tomato pulp or broken-up canned plum tomatoes
> 1 cup peeled and chopped potatoes
> 3 peppercorns
> 6 sprigs parsley

1. *If using meat:* Simmer the beef and bone in the water, or water and broth, with salt to taste if you wish, for 1 hour.
2. Lightly brown bacon in large, heavy pot. Remove bacon. Sauté onion and celery in the remaining fat until wilted and lightly colored.
3. Add the beef and bone (if you are using them), water, bacon, and all the remaining ingredients to the pot. Bring to a boil, then simmer, uncovered, for 45 minutes.
4. Remove solids. Separate the meat and bones from the vegetables. Strain the vegetables through finest disk of a food mill or sieve, or purée in a food processor. Return the vegetable purée to the broth. Reserve the meat for later.

for completing soup:

2 cups julienned or coarsely grated beets
1 cup julienned or coarsely grated carrots
4 tablespoons butter
3 cups shredded cabbage
Salt (if desired)
Freshly ground black pepper
Fresh lemon juice
Fresh chopped dill (optional)
Sour cream (optional)

1. Bring the prepared broth to a simmer.
2. In large, heavy pan or pot, sauté the beets and carrots in half the butter. Add to simmering soup base. DO NOT BOIL (see Note). Simmer for 15 minutes.
3. Add remaining butter to the sauté pan and braise cabbage, stirring occasionally, for 5 minutes or until wilted and slightly colored. Add to soup and simmer another 15 minutes.
4. Add salt and/or pepper to taste. Add enough lemon juice to give a slightly tart but not sour taste.
5. Serve topped with dill and/or sour cream. If looking for a lower-fat substitute for sour cream, low-fat buttermilk works better than yogurt for taste if not appearance. Black bread and sweet butter make an appropriate accompaniment, and can complete the meal.

Makes about 2–2 1/2 quarts.

NOTES. Other vegetables, such as parsnips, celeriac, beans, and turnips, may be used in the base as desired. To thicken the soup, mashed cooked potato can be added.

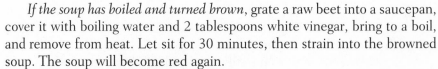

If the soup has boiled and turned brown, grate a raw beet into a saucepan, cover it with boiling water and 2 tablespoons white vinegar, bring to a boil, and remove from heat. Let sit for 30 minutes, then strain into the browned soup. The soup will become red again.

Traditionally, a Russian brew called *kvas* is used in preference to lemon juice. I find the prospect of making it daunting and I've never tried it. Here's the recipe; maybe you'll be brave.

Kvas

8–10 beets, peeled and chopped
Water
½ cup milk
2 slices bread (rye or whole wheat best)
Lukewarm water

1. Place beets in crock or wide-mouthed glass container. Cover with water, add milk, and top with bread.
2. Cover and keep in warm place until fermented. It will take anywhere from 24 hours to 3 days to ferment.
3. Strain and store in a glass container in refrigerator until ready to use. Will keep for a week or two.

To make a hearty dinner with borscht—which already has practically every vegetable in it, plus meat and carb (potato)—a traditional accompaniment is pierogi, which are like little loaves or buns baked around a morsel of filling. Since this is a late autumn and winter dish, a good dessert would be baked apple.

DINNER OR LATE SUPPER

Borscht (recipe above)

Pierogi (recipe follows)

Baked Apple

Pierogi or Pirozhki

dough

1 package yeast
¼ cup tepid water
1 cup milk
3½ cups sifted flour, or more
1 egg plus 1 white (reserve the yolk)
1 tablespoon sugar
1 teaspoon salt or less
2 tablespoons melted butter or oil

Preheat oven to 425°.

1. Put yeast in tepid water. Scald milk and cool to slightly more than room temperature. Add yeast mixture, plus half the flour, and blend until free of lumps. Cover and allow to work for 30 minutes or more.
2. Mix whole egg and white, sugar, salt, and butter or oil and add to yeast-flour mixture, which will sink. Add remaining flour until soft dough can be worked. Knead until very pliable and satiny, as much as 10 minutes.
3. Place the smoothed ball of dough in a greased bowl, turning to grease exposed top of dough, cover with a cloth, and let rise until doubled—about 1½ hours—in a warm spot (but not so warm that it starts cooking the yeast and killing it).

Pierogi can be filled with potatoes or combinations of vegetables. Here is a meat filling.

filling:

½ pound ground beef
6 tablespoons butter
2 medium onions, chopped
¾ cup beef broth (bouillon okay)
2 tablespoons flour
1 teaspoon salt or less
Freshly ground black pepper
2 tablespoons minced fresh parsley or dill

1. Brown meat in half the butter (3 tablespoons). Purée in a food mill or food processor until the meat is very finely chopped.

2. Using the rest of the butter, brown the onions. Deglaze the pan with broth.
3. Put the flour in a Pyrex measuring cup or small bowl and add the broth from the pan with pan juices a little at a time, stirring until smooth. Add the mixture to the pan with the onions and cook, stirring, until thickened.
4. Remove from the heat and mix in meat and seasonings.

to complete the pierogi:

1 egg yolk (reserved from above)
1 tablespoon water

1. Pull off knobs of dough and form into balls about 1½ inches in diameter. (The dough will sink.) Roll the balls out on a floured surface to make a pancake about ¼ inch thick and 3 inches across. Use about 1 teaspoon filling per round. Fold two sides over the filling as if folding a letter in thirds, leaving the ends open. Remember, they will expand. Place on a greased baking sheet, cover with a cloth, and allow to rise until puffy, about 20 minutes or longer.
2. Mix egg yolk with water and brush mixture over the folded dough, taking care not to squash it. Bake 15 minutes.
3. Lower the oven temperature to 400° and bake until lightly golden, another 20 minutes or so. The pierogi should be firm but slightly soft.

Or buy frozen pierogi in the supermarket. After all, you've already made the borscht.

Makes 20 to 25 pierogi.

FORBIDDEN FRUITS

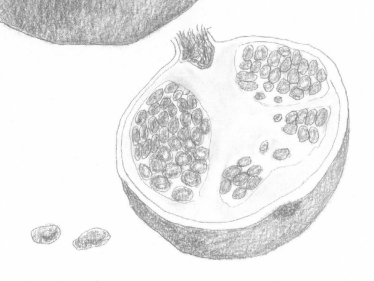

"THE POMEGRANATE SEEDS"

from TANGLEWOOD TALES

by Nathaniel Hawthorne

(1 8 5 3)

It is perhaps perverse, if you want to use a Greek myth in a cookbook at all, to use a version written by a nineteenth-century American: "The Pomegranate Seeds," from Nathaniel Hawthorne's *Tanglewood Tales*. But since the salient aspect of this myth is a fruit, this is definitely the version to choose, since Hawthorne's pomegranate is not just a symbol but a very particular, palpable pomegranate, a "wretched-looking pomegranate." In Hawthorne's version, a classic becomes a Transcendentalist allegory about the virtues of self-abnegation, compassion, and natural foods.

Persephone, here called Proserpina, has first of all disobeyed her wise mother, Ceres (as in "cereal"—she makes the crops grow, and all other plants), by wandering off alone, albeit in an innocent, childish game, unawares. She is kidnapped by the ruler of the underworld, here called King Pluto—that is, she is taken from the world of growing things into the world of death, the very opposite. Pluto offers her the water of forgetfulness from the river Lethe (to calm her horror) and anything else from his dead kingdom, but the girl just wants her old life back, and so finds herself engaged in a kind of unconscious ur-process of civil disobedience—a hunger strike—to get it. She doesn't know that accepting a host's food commits one to staying, according to the myth's rules; she just instinctively does the right thing.

When she is offered a cup of Lethe water, she declares in round, noble syllables, "I had a thousand times rather be miserable with remembering my mother, than be happy in forgetting her." Pluto has his cook whip up elaborate treats that elicit only, "I will neither drink that nor anything else . . . Nor will I taste a morsel of food, even if you keep me forever in your palace." Hawthorne goes on: "Now, if King Pluto had been cunning enough to offer

Proserpina some fruit or bread and milk (which was the simple fare to which the child had always been accustomed), it is very probable that she would soon have been tempted to eat it. But he left the matter entirely to his cook, who, like all other cooks, considered nothing fit to eat unless it were rich pastry, or highly seasoned meat, or spiced sweet cakes,—things which Proserpina's mother had never given her, and the smell of which quite took away her appetite, instead of sharpening it."

(The Transcendentalists—Emerson, Thoreau, Bronson Alcott, in whose circle Hawthorne moved—were among the early "food faddists," proto-hippies, fans of the strictest organic and vegetarian regimes and of living directly off the land without mercantile exchange. Some were followers of whole-grains advocate and minister Sylvester Graham, the progenitor of Graham crackers.)

The story of Persephone and the pomegranate is also a folk tale of how winter came to be. Until her daughter is found and returned to her, Ceres "had forbidden any fruits or vegetables to grow." When Pluto finally understands Proserpina's hippie health-food tendencies, he sends a servant to cater to them. But since nothing is growing, he can't find any organic food:

> After seeking all over the earth, King Pluto's servant found only a single pomegranate, and that so dried up as to be not worth eating. Nevertheless, since there was no better to be had, he brought this dry, old, withered pomegranate home to the palace, put it on a magnificent golden salver, and carried it up to Proserpina . . . To be sure, it was a very wretched-looking pomegranate, and seemed to have no more juice in it than an oyster-shell. But there was no choice of such things in King Pluto's palace. This was the first fruit she had seen there, and the last she was ever likely to see; and unless she ate it up immediately, it would grow drier than it already was, and be wholly unfit to eat.

So she capitulates. At almost the same moment, her mother finds her. After great rejoicing, Ceres asks her daughter if she ate while underground, knowing that to have done so will commit the girl to staying.

> "Dearest mother . . . I will tell you the whole truth. Until this very morning, not a morsel of food had passed my lips. But to-day, they brought me a pomegranate (a very dry one it was, and all shrivelled up, till there was little left of it but seeds and skin), and having seen no fruit for so long a time, and being faint with hunger, I was tempted just to bite it . . . I had not swallowed a morsel; but—dear mother, I hope it was no harm—but six of the pomegranate seeds, I am afraid, remained in my mouth."

"Ah, unfortunate child, and miserable me!" exclaimed Ceres. "For each of those six pomegranate seeds you must spend one month of every year in King Pluto's palace. You are but half restored to your mother. Only six months with me, and six with that good-for-nothing King of Darkness!"

For all of Hawthorne's appealing high-mindedness and nineteenth-century idealism, it is that "good-for-nothing" that exemplifies the light-hearted charm of the *Tanglewood Tales*. It is, enjoyably, just this side of ludicrous—and modern.

It is fitting that a tale of the onset of winter should pivot on a pomegranate. Though apples may seem more traditionally autumnal, in fact their harvest begins deep in summer, and they keep so beautifully that they could be eaten year-round, even in times before refrigeration and other more recent preservative technologies. If you live in a temperate climate, pomegranates appear in full autumn, and disappear by winter. Along with persimmons, they exemplify autumn, and make a perfect dessert combination if you are enough of a child of the Transcendentalists or other nature-lovers to care that your meals should reflect and even celebrate the local climate and changes of season.

The autumn fruits of the earth beginning with *p*—pumpkins, persimmons, pomegranates, and parsnips—go particularly well together. What follows is an adaptation of a medieval recipe for parsnips with pomegranates, and a recipe for persimmon pudding with pomegranates. Grenadine is pomegranate juice, so it would make a fitting addition to an autumn meal, mixed into seltzer, for instance. A fruit salad of sliced ripe persimmons with walnuts and pomegranate seeds, and cookies or ice cream on the side, is a supreme autumn dessert. Pumpkin pie would only be enhanced by a sprinkling of pomegranate seeds.

What most daunts people about pomegranates is getting the seeds out. Try to buy fruit that is deep red and has some give but is not at all wrinkled, hardened, or withered—"wretched-looking." Cutting downward from the crown, quarter it. Press each wedge with your thumbs against the outward curve of skin; it will pop inside-out. The membrane holding the seeds in place is then easily peeled away, and the seeds can be "sprung" from the pulp, over a bowl, scraping with the sides of your fingers to loosen them. The most important part of this operation is to wear either an apron or clothes you don't care about, or of a color that won't show the vivid sweet red of the juice, which is guaranteed to spurt.

The following dishes would round out a meal that includes kale or other late-fall greens cooked with onions and bacon fat or oil (you need fats in cold weather) and a pork dish or a savory beef-and-pumpkin pie such as the Beef Tart in *Ethan Frome*—ideal for one of those evenings when the sun goes down by five.

Parsnips with Pomegranate Seeds

Parsnips: size and amount to taste and need
Butter: 3 tablespoons per pound of parsnips; *or*
  Orange juice: ¼–½ cup per pound of parsnips
Pomegranate seeds: seeds from ½ pomegranate for each pound
  of parsnips

Preheat oven to 325°.

1. Butter a baking dish large enough to contain the parsnips in a single layer.
2. Peel the parsnips and place head to foot in the dish. Dot with butter, or add orange juice.
3. Bake up to 45 minutes, basting occasionally. The parsnips are done when pierced easily with a fork.
4. Sprinkle with pomegranate seeds and heat briefly. Serve.

NOTE: Parsnips are at their most delicious when pulled from the garden after the first frost or later, even into spring, for immediate cooking.

Persimmon Pudding

If you have never had Persimmon Pudding, it tastes something like Indian Pudding—comforting, substantial, and like a heavenly meal in itself.

1⅓ cups sifted flour
1 cup sugar
½ teaspoon baking soda
Pinch salt (optional)
½ teaspoon ginger
½ teaspoon cinnamon
½ teaspoon nutmeg
3 good-sized ripe persimmons, peeled, central pip removed
3 eggs, lightly beaten
1 quart milk
½ cup melted butter
Whipped cream (optional)
Pomegranate seeds (optional)

Preheat oven to 300°.

1. Sift the flour, sugar, baking soda, salt, ginger, cinnamon, and nutmeg together in bowl large enough to contain all ingredients later.
2. Purée the persimmons—you should have about 1 cup puréed pulp. Mix persimmon pulp with eggs, milk, and butter.
3. Add the wet ingredients to dry ingredients by small amounts, mixing after each addition.
4. Pour mixture into greased 13 × 9 × 2 inch pan or equivalent baking dish and bake, uncovered, about 1 hour, until a knife inserted near the center comes out clean. Serve warm, scattered with pomegranate seeds or accompanied by whipped cream—or both—if desired.

Serves 12.

NOTE: Raising the oven temperature 50 degrees or so as the pudding finishes cooking (when it looks done but tests unfirm at the center) can create a delicious crust. If you love crust (as I do), make this in a big, shallow pan to create a larger surface area.

LATE AUTUMN DINNER

Roast pork loin

Parsnips with Pomegranate Seeds (recipe above)

Potato chunks brown-roasted in film of olive oil*

Greens (kale, chard, etc.) sautéed with onions and fat

Persimmon Pudding (recipe above) with Butter Cookies**

*See note for potato recipe in *The Man Who Loved Children.*
**Recipe in *David Copperfield.*

"ROYAL BEATINGS"

from THE BEGGAR MAID

by Alice Munro

(1 9 7 7)

Food —and love—in Alice Munro's stories is almost always bound up with pain, humiliation, exhibiting oneself, and fear of exposure. Elaborate meals are prepared for lovers who never show up or call, or a character is secretly bulimic. There is a great deal of pleasurable female masochism, pleasure compulsively sought where the woman is sure to be shamed and betrayed—followed by a further pleasure in exhibiting the shame and betrayal, in being the kind of woman to whom this happens, sharing it with other women. Many of Munro's earlier stories concern a very bright, poor girl who grows up to be this sort of woman: well-educated through her own efforts, talented, successful, self-punishing, and unable to leave a harsh, deprived past behind. The definitive version may be Munro's story cycle *The Beggar Maid*, in which the pattern of all the heroine's future relationships seems to be laid out in the initial story, "Royal Beatings."

Her name is Rose. She lives with her somewhat withdrawn father and the woman he married when Rose was a baby, Flo, as well as a young half-brother, Brian. A small grocery store supports them—just. They live in a semi-rural slum in a sub-working-class community full of undisguised judgment and unforgivingness. The crucial scene describes the generic royal beating of the title.

The beating has its genesis in the always bad relations between Rose and Flo, which have only worsened as Rose, far outstripping Flo intellectually, reaches adolescence. The wrangle is described as having gone on "forever, like a dream that goes back and back into other dreams, over hills and through doorways, maddeningly dim and populous and familiar and elusive." On this occasion, Flo has decided to spend her Saturday scrubbing the kitchen floor, which makes her feel resentful and hard done by. The floor itself is a very in-carnation of their poverty and of poverty's inventiveness, having "five or six different patterns of linoleum on it. Ends, which Flo got for nothing and in-geniously trimmed and fitted together, bordering them with tin strips and tacks."

Rose knows that Flo is just looking for something to set her off, and Rose provides it by getting little Brian to recite verses that have always enraged Flo, who hates "filth":

> Two Vancouvers fried in snot!
> Two pickled arseholes tied in a knot!

Rose has deliberately gotten herself into trouble this way before:

> Rose couldn't stop herself. She hummed it tenderly, tried saying the innocent words aloud, humming through the others. It was not just the words snot and arsehole that gave her pleasure, though of course they did. It was the pickling and tying and the unimaginable Vancouvers. She saw them in her mind shaped rather like octopuses, twitching in the pan. The tumble of reason; the spark and spit of craziness.
>
> Lately she has remembered it again and taught it to Brian, to see if it has the same effect on him, and of course it has.

So Flo is already furious at hearing the old verses again, and from her son, as she begins scrubbing:

> What do they have to say to each other? It doesn't really matter. Flo speaks of Rose's smart-aleck behavior, rudeness and sloppiness and con-ceit. Her willingness to make work for others, her lack of gratitude. She mentions Brian's innocence, Rose's corruption. Oh, don't you think you're somebody, says Flo, and a moment later, Who do you think you are?

That phrase is the bane of Rose's existence. Because Rose is, in fact, ex-ceptional, she is treated as stuck-up. Disastrously, she defends herself by being smart—reasonable. This goads Flo on to the next stage of their repet-itive, age-old drama: calling Rose's father in. He knows his role perfectly too, naturally. "He is slow at getting into the spirit of things . . . won't look at Rose." He won't let her talk either, to defend herself from Flo's accusations; he needs to listen only to his wife to work himself up, and he might be in danger of being swayed by logic if he heard Rose.

He is beginning to warm up. He gives her a look. This look is at first cold and challenging. It informs her of his judgment, of the hopelessness of her position. Then it clears, it begins to fill up with something else, the way a spring fills up when you clear the leaves away. It fills with hatred and pleasure. Rose sees that and knows it. Is that just a description of anger, should she see his eyes filling up with anger? No. Hatred is right. Pleasure is right. His face loosens and changes and grows younger . . .

Then, the beating. By this time, Flo is having second thoughts: "Do you have to use the belt?"

He doesn't answer. The belt is coming off, not hastily. It is being grasped at the necessary point. *All right you.* He is coming over to Rose. He pushes her off the table. His face, like his voice, is quite out of character. He is like a bad actor, who turns a part grotesque. As if he must savor and insist on just what is shameful and terrible about this. That is not to say he is pretending, that he is acting, and does not mean it. He is acting, and he means it. Rose knows that, she knows everything about him . . .

She tries again looking at the kitchen floor, that clever and comforting geometrical arrangement, instead of looking at him or his belt. How can this go on in front of such daily witnesses—the linoleum, the calendar with the mill and creek and autumn trees, the old accommodating pots and pans?

Hold out your hand!

Those things aren't going to help her, none of them can rescue her. They turn bland and useless, even unfriendly. Pots can show malice, the patterns of linoleum can leer up at you, treachery is the other side of dailiness.

At the first, or maybe the second, crack of pain, she draws back. She will not accept it. She runs around the room, she tries to get to the doors. Her father blocks her off. Not an ounce of courage or of stoicism in her, it would seem. She runs, she screams, she implores. Her father is after her, cracking the belt at her when he can, then abandoning it and using his hands. Bang over the ear, then bang over the other ear. Back and forth, her head ringing. Bang in the face. Up against the wall and bang in the face again. He shakes her and hits her against the wall, he kicks her legs. She is incoherent, insane, shrieking. *Forgive me! Oh please, forgive me!*

Flo is shrieking too. *Stop, stop!*

Not yet. He throws Rose down. Or perhaps she throws herself down. He kicks her legs again. She has given up on words but is letting out a noise, the sort of noise that makes Flo cry, *Oh, what if people can hear*

49

her? The very last-ditch willing sound of humiliation and defeat it is, for it seems Rose must play her part in this with the same grossness, the same exaggeration, that her father displays, playing his. She plays his victim with a self-indulgence that arouses, and maybe hopes to arouse, his final, sickened contempt.

They will give this anything that is necessary, it seems, they will go to any lengths.

Not quite. He has never managed really to injure her, though there are times, of course, when she prays that he will. He hits her with an open hand, there is some restraint in his kicks.

Now he stops, he is out of breath. He allows Flo to move in, he grabs Rose up and gives her a push in Flo's direction, making a sound of disgust. Flo retrieves her, opens the stair door, shoves her up the stairs.

"Go on up to your room now! Hurry!"

Rose languishes in her room, hating them, but powerless. All this leads to the meal, which has all the attractiveness and destructive power of a taboo object.

. . . a tray will appear. Flo will put it down without a word and go away. A large glass of chocolate milk on it, made with Vita-Malt from the store. Some rich streaks of Vita-Malt around the bottom of the glass. Little sandwiches, neat and appetizing. Canned salmon of the first quality and reddest color, plenty of mayonnaise. A couple of butter tarts from a bakery package, chocolate biscuits with a peppermint filling. Rose's favorites, in the sandwich, tart and cookie line. She will turn away, refuse to look, but left alone with these eatables will be miserably tempted, roused and troubled and drawn back from thoughts of suicide or flight by the smell of salmon, the anticipation of crisp chocolate, she will reach out a finger, just to run it around the edge of one of the sandwiches (crusts cut off!) to get the overflow, get a taste. Then she will decide to eat one, for strength to refuse the rest. One will not be noticed. Soon, in helpless corruption, she will eat them all. She will drink the chocolate milk, eat the tarts, eat the cookies. She will get the malty syrup out of the bottom of the glass with her finger, though she sniffles with shame. Too late.

Flo will come up and get the tray. She may say, "I see you got your appetite still," or, "Did you like the chocolate milk, was it enough syrup in it?" depending on how chastened she is feeling, herself. At any rate, all advantage will be lost. Rose will understand that life has started up again, that they will all sit around the table eating again, listening to the radio news. Tomorrow morning, maybe even tonight. Unseemly and unlikely as that may be. They will be embarrassed, but rather less than you might expect considering how they have behaved. They will feel a queer lassitude, a convalescent indolence, not far off satisfaction.

Later in the story cycle, these comments are made about Flo: "It was love she sickened at. It was the enslavement, the self-abasement, the self-deception . . . readiness, need." Later still Munro adds that "there was not a thing in their lives they were protected from. Flo was there to see to that." Rose does far worse than Persephone in eating her modest treat—salmon sandwiches, with the crusts trimmed!—earning something like a whole lifetime of winter. In succumbing to the least pleasure, in being fool enough to accept the least version of love, Rose is condemned never to get the large version, and never to escape her childhood home, however great a success she is in the world (and she is), however far she flies, whatever great knowledge she accrues. In the "helpless corruption" of need, she is damned.

It is tempting to come up with a recipe for Vancouvers fried in snot or knotted pickled arseholes—definitely home cooking, not company meals. It is too dull to say how to make a salmon sandwich. However, there is a salmon spread that is as ambrosial as those sandwiches are to Rose. It is definitely company food, delicious served as an appetizer with crackers or small rounds of baguette-style bread—crusts on.

Salmon Loaf

1 6-ounce can good salmon, skin and bone remnants picked out
Juice of 1 lemon
1 8-ounce package cream cheese, softened
1 teaspoon grated horseradish
Lightly chopped pecans or walnuts, to cover (texture should be
    gravelly, not powdery)
Finely chopped fresh parsley, to cover (about the same amount
    as chopped nuts—a handful or two)

1. Mash salmon with lemon juice, softened cream cheese, and horseradish
   in bowl or food processor until smoothly blended. Refrigerate about
   1 hour or more.
2. Turn mixture onto a sheet of wax paper. Using the paper to shape it, form
   into a log or loaf. Wrap in the wax paper and refrigerate until firm (about
   20 minutes to 1 hour).
3. When the loaf is firm, open wax paper and tilt to roll the loaf to one side.
   Cover the remaining stretch of paper, now flat on the counter, with a mixture of nuts and parsley. Tilting the paper again the other way, carefully
   roll the loaf back across it, picking up as much of the nuts and parsley
   as possible. Continue rolling back and forth until the pink is covered in
   brown and green. Push extra mounds of parsley-nut mix against the two
   loaf ends with your fingers or a rubber scraper. Rewrap in the wax paper
   and replace in refrigerator until ready to serve.

HORS D'OEUVRES

Salmon Loaf (recipe above)

*Dry Salted Fare**

Baguette cut into thin rounds

Cherry tomatoes

Wine, beer, and cocktails or other drinks

*Crackers—recipe in *Moby-Dick.*

FROM HUNGER

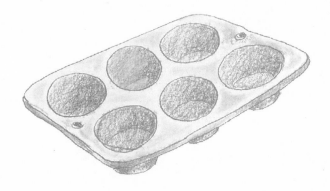

SERENADE

by James M. Cain

(1 9 3 7)

*I*n this short novel, Cain's patented tough-guy voice—the tone of an un-educated guy straining his patience to give out the straight dope to a pitiably less intelligent auditor—is put into the unlikely mouth of a world-class opera singer who is insecure about his sexuality. There's nothing John Howard Sharp, the singer, doesn't know more about than anybody else, so he's full of belligerent opinionizing, but he's also as down on his luck as he could be: his voice is shot, he's penniless, and stranded in Mexico City. The hotel where he was a paying guest is letting him stay on, however, not know-ing that he sneaks down to the kitchen at night:

> I found ten centavos in the street one day and bought a tin spoon, a clay soapdish, and a cake of soap. The soapdish and the soap I put on the washstand, like they were some improvements of my own I was putting in, since they wouldn't give me any. The spoon I kept in my pocket. Every night when I'd go down, I'd scoop beans, rice, or whatever they had, and sometimes a little meat into the soapdish, but only when there was enough that it wouldn't be missed. I never touched anything that might have counted, and only took off the top of dishes where there was quite a lot of it, and then smoothed them up to look right. Once there was half a Mexican ham in there. I cut myself off a little piece, under the butt.

In the opening scene, Sharp tries to pick up a woman in a bar. He buys her a lottery ticket, and she seems interested until, to demonstrate how much better he is than a mariachi singer, he grabs a guitar and bellows an air from *Carmen*. Juana loses interest, and he sees her face as "the face at the win-dow of every whorehouse in the world."

As it turns out, she is a whore—and, winning the *lotería* with the lucky ticket he bought her, wants to open a bordello in Acapulco with Sharp as the manager. He is in no position to say no to a job, so he goes with her in the fancy new car she has bought with her winnings, off into roadless, cactus-strewn Indian country, where Juana insists on stopping for supplies she's commissioned her mother to buy for the new venture. At her parents' doorless hut, they load the car down with, as Cain renders Juana's English, "good estoff":

> Papa ducked in there and began to carry out iron plates for cooking tortillas, machetes, pots, and jars and such stuff. One or two of them were copper, but most of them were pottery, and Mexican pottery means the worst pottery in the world. Then Mamma showed up with baskets of black beans, rice, ground corn, and eggs. I stowed the stuff in the rumble seat, shoving the pots in first. But pretty soon it was chock up to the top, and, when I came to the baskets I had to lash them to the side with some twine that they had so they rode the running board. Some of the stuff, like the charcoal, wasn't even in baskets. It was done up in bundles. I lashed that too. The eggs I finally found a place for in back, on top of her hatbox. Each egg was wrapped in cornhusk, and I figured they would ride all right there and not break.

Sharp draws the line, however, at live cargo—not only a burro, but the parents—whirling off with a protesting Juana into a whopping thunderstorm. They take refuge in an isolated church, occasioning fears of sacrilege in Juana. What follows is absolutely the high point of the book—all that I remembered ten years after first reading it, so that I thought of the book as wonderful. (The church interlude also contains the low point.) You won't be surprised that what goes on is a lot of food preparation.

First Sharp cooks some eggs on a stove improvised with tiles from the church floor and the charcoal. Then comes the low point. When Juana says his singing sounds like a priest, he is insulted and determined to prove his balls: "Yes, it was rape, but only technical, brother, only technical." As only happens in fiction, she loves it. They spend the next two days making love, eating eggs, and listening to the pouring rain. Then they wake up to sunshine, hungry, and see that the place is "alive with lizards."

To do this scene any justice at all, it must be quoted almost in its entirety. What makes it good is precisely the insane practical detail Cain goes into.

> I saw the evilest-looking thing I ever laid eyes on. It looked like some prehistoric monster you see in the encyclopedia, between two and three

feet long, with a scruff of spines that started at its head and went clear down its back, and a look in its eye like something in a nightmare. [Juana] had grabbed up a little tree that had washed out by the roots, and was closing in on him. "What are you doing? Let that goddam thing alone!"

When I spoke he shot out for the next rock like something on springs, but she made a swipe and caught him in mid-air. He landed about ten feet away, with his yellow belly showing and all four legs churning him around in circles. She scrambled over, hit him again, and then she grabbed him. "Machete! Quick, bring machete!"

"Machete, hell, let him go I tell you!"

"Is iguana! We cook! We eat!"

"Eat!—that thing?"

"The machete, the machete!"

He was scratching her by that time, and if she wouldn't let him go I wasn't letting him make hash out of her. I dove in the church for the machete. But then some memory of this animal caught me. I don't know whether it was something I had read in Cortés, or Diaz, or Martyr, or somebody, about how they cooked it when the Aztecs still ran Mexico, or some instinct I had brought away from Paris, or what. All I knew was that if we ever cut his head off he was going to be dead, and maybe that wouldn't be right. I didn't grab a machete. I grabbed a basket with a top on it, and dug out there with it. "The machete! The machete, give me machete!"

He had come to by now, and was fighting all he knew, but I grabbed him. The only place to grab him was in the belly on account of those spines on his back, and that put his claws right up your arm. She was bleeding up to her elbows and now it was my turn. Never mind how he felt and how he stunk. It was enough to turn your stomach. But I gave him the squeeze, shoved him headdown in the basket, and clapped the top on. Then I held it tight with both hands.

"Get some twine."

"But the machete! Why no bring—"

"Never mind. I'm doing this. Twine—string—that the things were tied with."

I carried him in, and she got some twine, and I tied the top on tight. Then I set him down and tried to think. She didn't make any sense out of it, but she let me alone. In a minute I fed up the fire, took the pot out and filled it with water. It had started to rain again. I came in and put the pot on to heat. It took a long while. Inside the basket those claws were ripping at the wicker, and I wondered if it would hold.

At last I got a simmer, and then I took the pot off and got another basket-top ready. I picked him up, held him way above my head, and dropped him to the floor. I remembered what shock did to him the first time, and I hoped it would work again. It didn't. When I cut the string and grabbed, I got teeth, but I held on and socked him in the pot. I whipped the basket-top on and held it with my knee. For three seconds it was like I had dropped an electric fan in there, but then it stopped. I took the top off and fished him out. He was dead, or as dead as a reptile ever gets. Then I found out why it was that something had told me to put him in the pot alive, and not cook him dead, with his head cut off, like she wanted to do. When he hit that scalding water he let go. He purged, and that meant he was clean inside as a whistle.

I went out, emptied the pot, heated a little more water, and scrubbed it clean with cornhusks, from the eggs. Then I scrubbed him off. Then I filled the pot, or about two thirds filled it, with clean water, and put it on the fire. When it began to smoke I dropped him in. "But is very fonny. Mamma no cook that way."

"Is fonny, but inspiration has hit me. Never mind how Mamma does it. This is how I do it, and I think it's going to be good."

I fed up the fire, and pretty soon it boiled. I cut it down to a simmer, and this smell began to come off it. It was a stink, and yet it smelled right, like I knew it was going to smell. I let it cook along, and every now and then I'd fish him up and pull one of his claws. When a claw pulled out I figured he was done. I took him out and put him in a bowl. She reached for the pot to go out and empty it. I almost fainted. "Let that water alone. Leave it there, right where it is."

I cut off his head, opened his belly, and cleaned him. I saved his liver, and was plenty careful how I dissected off the gall bladder. Then I skinned him and took off the meat. The best of it was along the back and down the tail, but I carved the legs too, so as not to miss anything. The meat and liver I stowed in a little bowl. The guts I threw out. The bones I put back in the pot and fed up the fire again, so it began to simmer. "You better make yourself comfortable. It's a long time before dinner."

I aimed to boil about half that water away. It began to get dark and we lit the candles and watched and smelled. I washed off three eggs and dropped them in. When they were hard I fished them out, peeled them, and laid them in a bowl with the meat. She pounded up some coffee. After a long time that soup was almost done. Then something popped into my mind. "Listen, we got any paprika?"

"No, no paprika."

"Gee, we ought to have paprika."

"Pepper, salt, yes. No paprika."

"Go out there to the car and have a look. This stuff needs paprika, and it would be a shame not to have it just because we didn't look."

"I go, but is no paprika."

She took a candle and went back to the car. I didn't need any paprika. But I wanted to get rid of her so I could pull off something without any more talk about the *sacrilegio*. I took a candle and a machete and went back of the altar. There were four or five closets back there, and a couple of them were locked. I slipped the machete blade into one and snapped the lock. It was full of firecrackers for high mass and stuff for the Christmas crèche. I broke into another one. There it was, what I was looking for, six or eight bottles of sacramental wine. I grabbed a bottle, closed the closets, and came back. I dug the cork out with my knife and tasted it. It was A-1 sherry. I socked about a pint in the pot and hid the bottle. As soon as it heated up a little I lifted the pot off, dropped the meat in, sliced up the eggs, and put them in. I sprinkled in some salt and a little pepper.

She came back. "Is no paprika."

"It's all right. We don't need it. Dinner's ready."

We dug in.

Well, brother, you can have your Terrapin Maryland. It's a noble dish, but it's not Iguana John Howard Sharp. The meat is a little like chicken, a little like frog-legs, and a little like muskrat, but it's tenderer than any of them. The soup is one of the great soups of the world, and I've eaten Marseilles bouillabaisse, New Orleans crayfish bisque, clear green turtle, thick green turtle, and all kinds of other turtle there are. I think it was still better that we had to drink it out of bowls, and fish the meat out with a knife. It's gelatinous, and flooding up over your lips, it makes them sticky, so you can feel it as well as taste it. She drank hers stretched out on her belly, and after a while it occurred to me that if I got down and stuck my mouth up against hers, we would be stuck, so we experimented on that for a while. Then we drank some more soup, ate some more meat, and made the coffee. While we were drinking that she started to laugh. "Yeh? And what's so funny?"

"I feel—how you say? Dronk?"

"Probably born that way."

"I think you find wine. I think you steal wine, put in iguana."

"Well?"

"I like, very much."

"Why didn't you say so sooner?"

So I got out the bottle, and we began to swig it out of the neck. Pretty soon we were smearing her nipples with soup, to see if they would stick. Then after a while we just lay there, and laughed.

What follows is a long anticlimax. Sharp doesn't like the way Juana is treated by the "politico" who is using his influence for her whorehouse in Acapulco, and Sharp decks the guy. This makes Sharp a fugitive. He strikes up a convenient acquaintance with a ship's captain and wangles a berth for himself and Juana. The captain likes them so much he smuggles her into California. As a result of having sex with Juana, Sharp has his voice back—yes, that's how it works here—and on that basis negotiates a Hollywood contract. Because he knows more than everybody, including the director and producer of the first movie he makes, he masterminds how to turn it into a hit. It's such a big hit, in fact, that he is offered a contract with the Metropolitan Opera in New York, so he breaks his Hollywood contract and they go east. Sharp takes on a radio show on the side; money is not, to say the least, a problem. Contract troubles, however, are. A seeming good angel appears, a hugely wealthy man who can tell the movie producers and radio bigwigs where to get off. Juana, with her mystical Mexican Indian powers, sees something else: that the wealthy man, Winston Hawes, is homosexual; that Sharp is afraid of him; and that Sharp and Winston once were lovers—and that that was why Sharp lost his voice. Juana does her best to save his career and, by her lights, his manhood. It involves eating . . . in a sense:

> All of a sudden she broke from me, shoved the dress down from her shoulder, slipped the brassiere and shoved a nipple in my mouth. "Eat. Eat much. Make big *toro!*"
> "I know now, my whole life comes from there."
> "Yes, eat."

Well, now you know more than you ever wanted to about the cranky clutter of Cain's conventional, limited mind. From here, Sharp lapses into an almost sensual passivity, leaving everything to Juana. There are a couple of murders. He ends up as he began, alone in Mexico, but this time, never likely to sing again.

I don't know where I could come up with a dish that would equal Iguana John Howard Sharp—and I don't know where you can pick up an iguana. Perhaps you could try Sharp's recipe substituting the chicken or frog's legs to which he unfavorably compares his beloved ig-Juana (muskrat would presumably be as difficult to get hold of as the lizard). But the real essence seems to be the sensuality and improvisatory whimsicality of the dish. For that, there is a classical Mexican recipe. No paprika required, but it does use hard-boiled eggs. It is a kind of stew cooked inside a cheese, and can be eaten with one's fingers—especially if they are holding a tortilla.

Stuffed Edam (Queso Relleno)

This recipe looks long and complicated. It does have many ingredients, but it is not at all difficult. Keep in mind that it is made in three or four distinct steps: simmering the meat, sautéing the vegetables for the stuffing, steaming the stuffed cheese (being very careful not to let the wonderful head shape become a gooey glob), and assembling the gravy.

outer portion

1 4-pound Edam cheese
Oil
Cheesecloth

stuffing

1½ pounds pork, cut in ½-inch cubes
3 cloves garlic, mashed
1 teaspoon dried oregano
½ teaspoon salt or less
3 cups water
2 tablespoons oil
1 small onion, minced
½ small green pepper, minced
1 large tomato, peeled and puréed, or 1 cup canned
    tomato purée
12 green olives, pitted and chopped
1 tablespoon capers
1 tablespoon raisins
1 jalapeño chili, washed and seeds removed, minced
1 tablespoon red wine vinegar

continued

10 peppercorns
2 cloves
Salt
4 eggs, hard-boiled

sauce

1 large peeled tomato, puréed, or 1 cup canned tomato purée
Pinch saffron
2 tablespoons flour

1. Place pork, garlic, oregano, and salt in a pot with the water and simmer, covered, about a half hour, until meat feels tender. Remove meat from broth, reserving the broth. Mince pork.
2. Peel the wax from the cheese and cut a ½-inch slice cleanly off the top, like a jack-o'-lantern lid. Hollow out the body of the cheese, leaving ½-inch-thick walls.
3. Remove hard-boiled yolks intact from whites. They will be used whole. Chop whites.
4. Heat oil in pan and sauté onion and pepper until lightly browned. Add tomato, olives, capers, raisins, chili, chopped egg whites, and vinegar. Grind the peppercorns with the cloves in a mortar, and add. Add pork and heat through. Salt to taste. (Remember the olives will also be salty.)
5. Scoop about half of the stuffing mixture from pan into the hollowed cheese. Place egg yolks around the surface. Add the remaining stuffing mixture and replace cheese lid.
6. Generously oil outside of cheese. Wrap it in cheesecloth and place it in a steamer over boiling water. Steam at medium heat for about 15 minutes or less. The cheese should soften and start spreading. Be very careful to heat the cheese only until it is *just barely soft* or it will melt into the cheesecloth.
7. Reheat reserved pork broth and add the second cup of tomato purée and saffron. Remove ½ cup of the hot mixture and beat with flour. When smooth, return thickened mixture to pot and whisk. Sauce should thicken slightly.
8. Remove the cheesecloth and place the cheese on a platter. Pour the sauce over it. Remove the lid. May be served surrounded by 16 to 20 warm corn tortillas, or, as an entrée, with rice, or both.

Serves 18 as an appetizer, 6 as an entrée.

MEXICAN DINNER OR BRUNCH

Stuffed Edam with tortillas (recipe above)

Yellow rice (white rice with saffron or cumin)

*Mixed greens with tomatoes, baby corn, fresh cilantro, and
Vinaigrette**

Café con Leche (recipe follows)

Fried bananas or fresh mango with chopped mint leaves

Café con Leche

1 quart water
¼ cup brown sugar
½ stick cinnamon
⅔ cup French roast, Bustelo, or other dark, finely ground coffee
1 quart milk
Ground cinnamon (optional)
Chocolate shavings (optional)

1. Heat water with sugar and cinnamon stick, stirring until sugar is dissolved.
2. Add the coffee. Simmer 4 to 5 minutes, or to taste. Pour through a fine strainer or coffee filter, making sure liquid stays hot.
3. Heat milk. Fill each cup halfway with hot coffee, then fill the remainder with milk. (If you want the milk frothy, as with cappuccino, whisk or beat the hot milk before pouring it into cups.) Serve immediately, sprinkled with cinnamon or chocolate shavings if desired.

Easily serves 8, or 10 if cups rather than mugs are used.

*Recipe in *The Sweet Dove Died.*

"BONTSHE SHVAYG"

by I. L. Peretz

(1 8 9 4)

Translated by Hillel Halkin

Bontshe Shvayg, or Bontshe the Silent, is a man who endures a life of injustice, mistreatment, privation, and indignity with "Not one word against God. Not one word against man." Unlike even Job, he never cries out:

He was born in silence. He lived in silence. He died in silence. And he was buried in a silence greater yet.

No one knows what he died of—"he might have starved to death"—though he died in a hospital. No wine was drunk at his bris or bar mitzvah, and even the wooden sign marking his grave is used by the gravedigger's wife for a fire to boil potatoes. His stepmother fed him moldy bread and gristle as a child "while she herself drank coffee with cream in it." His father as well is defined by what he ingests: "A drunk."

Bontshe saves a rich Jew. He is rewarded with a job and the man's mistress. She turns out to have been carrying the rich man's bastard, whom Bontshe takes on. The rich man fails to pay him, though, and even the boy grows up to throw Bontshe out.

You learn these things as Bontshe is welcomed into heaven, where his deeds are being judged by the heavenly tribunal. The very prosecutor can find nothing to prosecute: "*He* kept silent. I will do the same." The judge finally is ready with his judgment.

"My child . . . you have suffered all in silence. There is not an unbroken bone in your body, not a corner of your soul that has not bled. And you have kept silent.

"There, in the world below, no one appreciated you. You yourself never knew that had you cried out but once, you could have brought down the walls of Jericho. You never knew what powers lay within you.

"There, in the World of Deceit, your silence went unrewarded. Here, in the world of Truth, it will be given its full due.

"The Heavenly Tribunal can pass no judgment on you. It is not for us to determine your portion of paradise. Take what you want! It is yours, all yours!"

Bontshe looked up for the first time. His eyes were blinded by the rays of light that streamed at him from all over. Everything glittered, glistened, blazed with light: the walls, the benches, the angels, the judges. So many angels!

He cast his dazed eyes down again. "Truly?" he asked, happy but abashed.

"Why, of course!" the judge said. "Of course! I tell you, it's all yours. All heaven belongs to you. Ask for anything you wish; you can choose what you like."

"Truly?" asked Bontshe again, a bit surer of himself.

"Truly! Truly! Truly!" clamored the heavenly host.

"Well, then," smiled Bontshe, "what I'd like most of all is a warm roll with fresh butter every morning."

The judges and angels hung their heads in shame. The prosecutor laughed.

I once tried to teach this story for a writing workshop, and embarrassed my class and myself by crying. It was a simple story, but simply heartbreaking. Its special heartbreak for a writer is the very silence at its core, speechlessness being the opposite of a profession devoted to articulation. But I also find that the more I look at this story, the less simple it is.

Read casually, it is like a Jewish folk tale, straightforwardly religious; about a Jesus figure though—Jesus as a shnook. Bontshe is totally good, like Jesus—heaven has seen nothing like him—but in a passive way. He is meekness itself; he asks nothing for himself, though he does look out for others (the rich Jew, the wife who was the rich man's mistress, the baby). His lack of complaint bespeaks a faith that wrongs are to be expected in the wicked world. Psychologically, it has a terrible truth. You feel Bontshe's sense of his own worthlessness: never having been given anything, including love, he neither expects nor feels that he deserves anything. His silence looks less like a virtue in that light, though more painful. He can ask only for the modest roll and butter because he can't imagine himself as deserving the jewels and riches and opulence being offered him. You start fantasizing (or I do): What *was* his relationship with his adopted son, that the boy at fifteen would throw him out? Was Bontshe merely dutiful but affectless, unable to show love and therefore unable to elicit it? In heaven, before Bontshe is offered his choice of all that is celestial, he hears what one presumes is the voice of the mother who died when he was a baby, calling to him with love. He wants to open his eyes, but "his tears had sealed them shut." Not just his mouth but his eyes are dammed. He is denied everything.

This is not a simple Jewish folk tale, nor is it primarily about the psychology of oppression and poverty. Peretz, a believing Jew in nineteenth-century Poland, was also a socialist. That is why, "had you cried out but once, you could have brought down the walls of Jericho." Clearly, Peretz thought that you should have enough faith in the creatures made in God's image, and capable of receiving God's word, to act in the world, and not merely be acted upon. The old-fashioned spelling-out that is a "moral" might be: if you don't ask for anything on earth, don't expect compensation even from heaven.

But why the angels and judges hang their heads in shame, one doesn't know. They may be ashamed for Bontshe—you are supposed to fear God, but you are supposed to trust God too; or ashamed at how little they are helping their protégé; or ashamed, even, of their own relative greed as they consider what they would have asked for (if angels can have desires, that is); or ashamed that their saint is so puny—the laughing prosecutor may be laughing at them. Or he may be laughing at the sheer incongruity of balancing a life of hardship and victimization with a hot roll and butter.

On the other hand, a life—or afterlife—in which a hot roll with butter appears "every morning" is likely to have other comforts to recommend it.

If I didn't have to go to the trouble of making it in the morning, because it was going to be supernaturally produced like Bontshe's breakfast roll, a popover would be my idea of heaven. At a restaurant in New York where popovers are served with most dishes, they come with a pot of strawberry butter. Mixing jam with soft butter is easy to do. Unlike Bontshe, you will have sweetness as well as richness.

Popovers

1 cup sifted flour
½ teaspoon salt
2 eggs
1 cup milk
1 tablespoon vegetable oil

Preheat oven to 425°.

1. Preheat muffin tin, tall custard cups, or popover pan (the sides must be higher than width of cup).
2. Combine all ingredients and beat or whip until smooth.
3. Very thoroughly grease hot cups.
4. Fill cups one-third full and bake about 35 minutes. Do not open oven earlier to check (you may cause the popped rolls to collapse). The sides should not be flexible to touch when done.

Makes 6 to 8 Popovers.

Jam-Butter

1 tablespoon softened butter
1 tablespoon jam, jelly, or preserves

Mash together with fork or whisk; or in blender, mixer, or food processor.

For 8 Popovers, you may want to triple this amount.

BREAKFAST

Coffee, Tea,* milk

Popovers (recipe above)

Jam-Butter (recipe above)

Strawberries, melon, grapefruit, or oranges

Fresh-squeezed fruit juice

*Recipe in *The Diary of a Good Neighbour.*

PENITENTIAL
MEALS

"JULIE DE CARNEILHAN"

by Colette

(1 9 4 1)

Translated by Patrick Leigh Fermor

Th is novella-length story is about a woman who, in seeking to gratify herself, punishes herself in everything. She is a middle-aged aristocratic divorcée fallen upon hard times, or harder times than they used to be. Julie, la Comtesse de Carneilhan, lives in a Paris apartment so inadequate that the toilet is in the kitchen. The story involves her in an intrigue with her second ex-husband, Herbert Espivant, a man who cheats her emotionally and finally financially, and cheated on her for the eight years they were married. The two decide to conspire against Espivant's very rich current wife to get a lump of money, which they are to split. The heart of the tale is not the money but Julie's pain over Herbert and the feeling that she cannot resist him in anything. Colette wrote elsewhere that few things are worse than to recall past happiness in present misery. At forty-five, Julie sees her life as finished in many of the ways that count, as though its second half will be little but penitence for how she lived the first.

At the beginning of the story, however, Julie is confident, coping, apparently heart-whole if somewhat heartless. This state is presented in the very first paragraph by way of—what else?—a meal:

> Mme. de Carneilhan turned off the gas, leaving the earthen-ware saucepan on the stove. Beside the stove she laid out the Empire teacup, the Swedish spoon and the rye-bread folded in a rough silk Turkish napkin. The smell of hot chocolate made her [stomach] yawn with hunger, for she had not eaten much for luncheon—a cold pork cutlet, a slice of bread and butter, half a pound of red currants and a cup of excellent coffee.

Most of us would not have considered that lunch light, but most of us are not aristocrats, sleeping on real linen, however worn, or hiring a housekeeper for our one-by-two-inch apartment. When the housekeeper asks what Julie wants for lunch the next day, Julie frivolously replies that she'd like "cream cheese and skate in black butter. The black and white together would look particularly smart." Still longing for the rapport she had with her reprobate of a husband, Julie all but moans when the meal is prepared, "I only thought I was saying something funny. You can eat your wretched skate. But leave me the cream cheese."

She is relieved of having to deal with it by the unexpected invitation from the wicked ex to lunch with him in his sickroom in the huge, elegant house that used to be hers, driven there by a chauffeur who knows her so well that he can state her very age (or nearly: he says forty-four). In contrast to the "frightful" skate, everything Julie is offered at Espivant's is alluring. She cheats herself of a good meal, however, in trying to pretend she's well enough off to scorn it: "Who asked for this ham, Herbert? Nobody wants it," she lies through her excellent teeth. She requests only fruit and coffee.

> . . . two tables laden with fruit were wheeled in. Julie found it all fault-less: late cherries, rose-colored peaches, thin-skinned Marseilles figs, cloudy hot-house grapes that had been carefully protected from the wasps. Iced water and champagne trembled in thick cut-glass jugs, chis-elled with a pattern of nail-heads. Julie's nostrils opened wide to the fumes of the coffee and the smell of the yellow rose standing next to a pot of fresh cream. She carefully concealed the pleasure she derived from all this luxury.

If Julie were not so amply self-loving and therefore all too capable of feeling sorry for herself, one would have to feel sorry for her here. A few pieces of fruit are a *very* light lunch.

Especially for someone who is actually sometimes going hungry, when the alimony check from husband number one is due:

> . . . she always dreaded, during these difficult last days of the month, her punctual and ineluctable yearnings for food. Spurned and postponed by endless cigarettes on an empty stomach, these yearnings came back again to torment her digestion. Julie had broken herself in to every kind of diet and could cope with anything except hunger.

Anything except lack of pretty clothes or lack of a lover, anyway, though she could hardly care less about the one she has—"A decent young industrialist with big childish eyes" called, ridiculously, Coco Vatard.

Delighted to be conspiring with her vile old husband, who will remind informed readers of Colette's infamous real-life husband, Willy, Julie sensually enjoys the meals she has while anticipating the extra money their plan will yield: a dinner of Beef Perigord, cheese, fruit, rolls, almonds in the shell, and "boiling" coffee; a breakfast of buckwheat pancakes and cider; a "well-chosen" steak, " 'As thick,' she thought, 'as a dictionary.' " But it ends badly, of course. Espivant has used her and cheated her, as he always has—he takes almost all the money. And he's managed to humiliate her as he always has, with another woman—his present wife comes calling in all her fabled exquisiteness. Julie, sick of "Three, four years of improvised meals on a card-table—'Delicious, these radishes with mustard. Julie's really *full* of ideas!' " she scornfully thinks—decides to return to the impoverished Carneilhan estate in the country; eating, the night before she takes off,

> another of her scratch meals, with soup and meat replaced by sardines and cheese. She sprinkled sugar on yesterday's fruit which was beginning to shrivel, but she felt defeated by the thought of making coffee.

Each morsel of food documents Julie's fallen state. This is yet another of those lonely, penitential meals that crop up with such distressing and conspicuous frequency in the work of women writers; a celebration, despite all her vivid sensual glory, of the heartache Colette often seems to consider woman's truest estate: punishment for having loved unwisely and too well.

H o t chocolate is penitential under no circumstances, unless you are allergic to chocolate. Unlike us, the French do not regard it as a children's consolation for not being allowed coffee, or as something solely for days spent playing in snow. (It has a caffeine-like substance in it anyway, so it is no better for a kid than café-au-lait—or Coke.) The French also don't, so far as I know, stick marshmallows into it. The very best hot chocolate, which can be served as a dessert more or less on its own—though some plain, delicate cookies would be nice by its side—is the stuff of its name: hot, melted chocolate. With milk. If you are really decadent, you can add cream or an egg; in Mexico, hot chocolate almost always comes with cinnamon. (The best powdered chocolate I've encountered is Mexican; it comes in an octagonal box with the Virgin Mary on it, and cinnamon in it.)

I name the recipe in tribute to the boyfriend Julie can hardly be bothered with, who is both sweet and rich, if soporific.

Cocoa Vatard

2 ounces unsweetened baker's chocolate
2 cups milk
1 cup heavy cream, or 1 additional cup milk
2–4 tablespoons sugar, to taste

1. Melt chocolate gently in double boiler.
2. Heat milk and cream together in separate pot; do not boil.
3. Add milk mixture to chocolate very slowly, stirring continuously, and making sure the mixture is well blended with each addition. Stir in sugar until dissolved.

Serves 3 or 4.

NOTE: This may be spiced with cinnamon or vanilla, sprinkled with unsweetened-chocolate shavings or powder or powdered espresso, or topped with the traditional whipped cream.

If you want the hot chocolate thicker or richer, pour a tiny bit into a bowl with a raw egg, beat together, then pour the mixture back into the pot of hot chocolate and whip. Using less milk yields a darker, more chocolatey blend. For breakfast, the plain hot chocolate-and-milk is perfect for dunking bread or rolls.

I'm afraid our French Julie gets a Mexican meal, just because cocoa is so traditional a dessert with fine Mexican cooking.

MEXICAN DINNER

Picadillo (recipe follows)

Humitas (recipe follows)

Rice

Refried black beans

Cocoa Vatard (recipe above)

Butter Cookies*

*Recipe in David Copperfield.

Picadillo

The combination of savory and sweet in Picadillo is so delicious that one is liable to eat until the stomach hurts.

  3 tablespoons oil
  2 pounds shredded or ground beef
  1 cup chopped onion
1–2 cloves garlic, minced
  1 cup canned or fresh tomatoes, peeled, seeded, drained, and
     chopped
  2 cooking apples, chopped, peeled, and cored
  3 jalapeño chilis, seeded, rinsed, and cut into ⅛-inch strips
  ½ cup raisins
10 pimiento-stuffed green olives, halved
  ⅛ teaspoon cinnamon
  ⅛ teaspoon ground cloves
  1 teaspoon salt, or to taste
Freshly ground black pepper
  ½ cup slivered almonds, toasted in oven till lightly browned

1. Heat oil and brown the beef thoroughly.
2. Add the onions and garlic, lower heat, and cook until the onions are transparent. Add the tomatoes, apples, chilis, raisins, olives, and spices. Just barely simmer, over very low heat, about 20 minutes, stirring now and then.
3. Sprinkle with almonds before serving, or place the almonds in a bowl on the table as a garnish.

Serves 4 to 6.

Humitas

4 cups corn
⅓ cup milk
2 eggs
2 teaspoons paprika
½ teaspoon salt, or to taste
Freshly ground black pepper
¼ cup butter
½ cup scallions, chopped
¼ cup green pepper, chopped
⅓ cup freshly grated Parmesan cheese

1. Purée corn with milk. Add the eggs, paprika, salt, and pepper and whip, or blend in a food processor.
2. In a pan large enough to accommodate all ingredients, melt butter, let foam subside, and then sauté scallions and green pepper until wilted. Add corn mixture and simmer uncovered, stirring, for 5 to 7 minutes.
3. When mixture is moderately thickened, remove from heat and stir in cheese to melt.

Serves 4 to 6.

THE SWEET DOVE DIED

by Barbara Pym

(1 9 7 8)

T*he* "delicious 'little something' " constantly produced by the heroine of *The Sweet Dove Died* for the man she loves charts the progress of their relationship. Food, in fact, is the occasion for demonstrating Leonora Eyre's relation to almost every character, even passing strangers. This sad, rigorous, and almost perfectly written book was produced when Pym, the author of six published novels, had given up on ever finding her work in print again, her seventh having been universally rejected. Maybe the prospect of having no audience to please freed her artistically, because *Dove,* her ninth, is surely better than everything that came before it except *Quartet in Autumn,* the eighth. (Which of the two is absolutely her best depends on which one you've read most recently.) At its center is a character Pym makes no attempt to render sympathetic: Leonora is cold, selfish, vain, a snob—anything except actively evil or wicked (she could hardly be bothered). Yet you don't dislike her; in fact, you are a rare and lucky person if, by the end, you do not see yourself in Leonora Eyre.

The action is simple enough: an uncle and a nephew, antiques dealers, meet Leonora at an auction. Both admire her. She is the "right" age for the uncle, but she likes the nephew. Oh, not "that way": sex has been something the beautiful Leonora only put up with occasionally; she just wants James around. And he, maybe gay, maybe not, in his early twenties, with an adored mother recently dead, more or less reciprocates, but does have sex—with others. Meanwhile, Leonora entertains the uncle's attentions to a point—at least to the point where he's a useful escort.

Leonora also has a pathetic friend—she prefers her female friends woebegone—whom she can pity for her hopeless adoring tolerance of a young homosexual man (not nearly of James's toniness). Dining with the two of them on a meal the friend has adoringly prepared, Leonora reacts to the man's teasing "about the way to a man's heart being through his stomach": "As if the question arose," Leonora thinks "scornfully." Yet it is only eleven pages later that Leonora herself is whisking together an impromptu meal for the gorgeous James, who is unexpectedly at her house—"pâté, salad and an omelette." As their odd relationship edges onto firmer ground, she's planning ahead so she can provide surprise treats to pioneer that alimentary route to affection: " 'Asparagus!' he exclaimed, as she came out of the kitchen with a dish. 'The first this year.' " She is, if anything, too successful. When James thinks of her, he thinks

> even more of the delicious "little something", always ready or made in a moment, that she invariably produced whenever one called on her.

As she loses heart over the relationship—she has learned of James's involvement with a young woman—she feels an unexpected, probably unwelcome solidarity with a stranger:

> She was carrying a shopping bag full of books, on top of which lay the brightly coloured packet of a frozen "dinner for one." Leonora could see the artistically delineated slices of beef with dark brown gravy, a little round of Yorkshire pudding, two mounds of mashed potato and brilliantly green peas. Her first feeling was her usual one of contempt for anybody who could live in this way, then, perhaps because growing unhappiness had made her more sensitive, she saw the woman going home to a cosy solitude, her dinner heated up in twenty-five minutes with no bother of preparation, books to read while she ate it . . .

Still, Leonora is so set on James that even when she cooks for his uncle, Humphrey, it is the nephew who is on her mind:

> She had cooked his favourite dishes: chicken with tarragon and chocolate mousse. It was not until she offered the latter and Humphrey refused it that she remembered that he hated anything chocolate. It was James who loved chocolate mousse.

One image captures with sharpness and resonance both Leonora's despair and the futility of her efforts:

> She leaned against the edge of a shelf, her forehead resting on the tins— prawns and lobster, asparagus tips, white peaches—that she always kept in case James should call unexpectedly for a meal.

By the end, as you may guess from this simplified retelling, Leonora is in much the same position as her pitiful friend. James meets a young man he becomes *very* interested in and neglects Leonora, even guiltily snubbing her at his mischievous lover's urging. Then he himself is dropped by the lover. When at last he visits Leonora again, ashamed but hopeful, she thinks of the wine her friend always keeps for these inevitable occasions, the favorite wine of her friend's young man.

> . . . there was something humiliating about the idea of wooing James in this way, like an animal being enticed back into its cage. Even if he had had a favourite wine, Leonora did not think she could have brought herself to produce it. Yet the sherry they were drinking now seemed actively hostile in its dryness, inhibiting speech and even feeling. If she had chosen something with a more festive air, something sweet or sparkling or warm—even a late cup of tea—would it have made any difference?

The story is resolved not with food but with flowers. I won't give away the ending. Here, however, is that chicken tarragon, which is made very nearly "in a moment," and is elegant besides. Likewise, chocolate mousse may be easier to make than you think. But even this most alluring of desserts will not make someone love you if they don't anyway.

Almost, though.

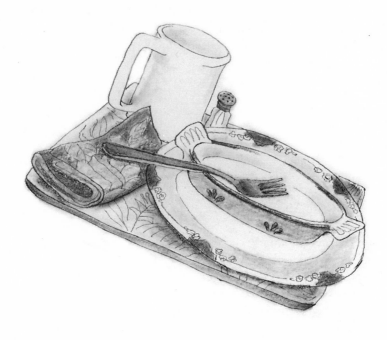

Chicken Breasts with Tarragon

3 whole chicken breasts, skinned, boned, and halved
Salt and freshly ground black pepper
¼ cup flour
¼ cup butter
1 tablespoon chopped shallots or onion
¼ cup dry white wine (Bordeaux preferred)
1 teaspoon chopped fresh tarragon, or ½ teaspoon dried
¼ cup chicken broth
¼ cup heavy cream

1. Sprinkle the chicken breasts with salt and pepper and dredge with flour. Reserve remaining flour.
2. In a large skillet, heat 3 tablespoons of the butter, add the chicken, and brown on both sides, slowly. Transfer to a heated platter. Add the shallots to the skillet and sauté briefly. Add the wine.
3. Cook the liquid over high heat until nearly evaporated, while scraping loose all the brown particles.
4. Add the reserved flour and stir to make a thick paste. Sprinkle with tarragon and stir in the chicken broth.
5. Return the chicken to the skillet, cover, and cook until tender, over very low heat, about 25 minutes. (High heat will make the meat tough.) Transfer the chicken to the platter and keep warm.
6. Add the remaining butter and the cream to the sauce in the skillet; heat, over moderate flame or coil setting, stirring, then pour the sauce over the chicken.

Serves 4 to 6.

Chocolate Mousse

¼ pound sweet chocolate
3 large eggs, separated
1½ tablespoons water
⅛ cup Grand Marnier, Amaretto, or Chartreuse
1 cup heavy whipping cream (not ultrapasteurized)

3 tablespoons sugar
Optional garnishes:
Whipped cream
Grated chocolate

1. Cut chocolate into ½-inch pieces and place in a saucepan or top of double boiler. Set the pan in hot, almost boiling water and cover. Turn heat down to low and allow contents to melt.
2. Put the egg yolks in a heavy saucepan and add the water, beating with wire whisk over low heat or boiling water until yolks are viscous. Add liqueur. Keep beating until mixture is just stiff enough to hold the mark of whisk for a moment or two before the lines dissolve.
3. Add the melted, still-warm chocolate to the yolks and fold it in. Scrape the sauce into a mixing bowl.
4. Beat cream until stiff, adding 2 tablespoons of the sugar toward the end. Fold into chocolate sauce.
5. Beat egg whites into soft peaks. Beat in remaining sugar and continue beating until the mixture is stiff. Fold into chocolate-cream mixture.
6. Spoon the mousse into a crystal bowl or individual serving bowls and chill. Garnish with whipped cream or grated chocolate before serving, if desired.

Serves 4 to 6.

This is a lot of main course and dessert for just two people, but what do you care? You're in love. And if it's unrequited, this will give you something to weep into as you console yourself with leftovers.

DINNER

Chicken Breasts with Tarragon (recipe above)

Tricolor rice (mixture of white, red, brown)

Sliced carrots with cinnamon and dash of maple syrup

Salad of baby greens, pine nuts, and Vinaigrette (recipe follows)

Chocolate Mousse (recipe above)

Vinaigrette

This isn't really a recipe. Vinaigrettes have to be made to taste, and tested with a leaf or other ingredient from your salad at that. But my basic ingredients (listed by proportion, biggest first) are almost always:

Virgin olive oil
Balsamic vinegar, or the finest red wine vinegar
Dash of Worcestershire sauce
Dash of soy sauce
Dash of Tabasco

You can vary the proportions to suit the salad. Some people like as much vinegar as oil. I generally have oil predominate by as much as three-quarters or even more. You can add mustard (powdered or prepared), mustard seeds, crushed or minced garlic, fresh herbs, dried herbs, shallots, parsley; you can add cream or sour cream; curry; buttermilk. Some people want more salt than the soy sauce provides, or instead of soy. A bit of sugar can brighten some salads, or you can make a sweet dressing using more sugar, or honey, especially if you switch to rice vinegar and a lighter oil. The beaten yolk of a fresh organic egg can enrich the dressing, and even take it halfway toward flavored mayonnaise.

Whisk the ingredients together in a small bowl or use fork, food processor, or blender. If no egg is used, ingredients can be shaken together in a jar, or mashed and stirred in a mortar and pestle. If you have time, it is good to let your vinaigrette sit a while before serving to let the flavors blend and "bloom."

FOOD OF LOVE

DAVID COPPERFIELD

by Charles Dickens

(1 8 5 0)

A *pivotal* concern with food tends to disappear in happy circumstances; food plays a more crucial role in an atmosphere of privation. This book, narrated by the title character, begins with his birth and
proceeds through his early, unthriving career and an early, unthriving marriage, on to maturity and better conditions. During David's unthriving ap-
prenticeship, he attempts to give a dinner party in his rented rooms for the
Micawbers, a couple comically impoverished and always running some harm-
less (and usually bootless) scam. In that spirit, Micawber copes with the in-
adequacies of David's domestic arrangements, which include an inept
landlady-cook and worse hired servant. Also present is David's friend Traddles.

I informed Mr. Micawber that I relied upon him for a bowl of punch,
and led him to the lemons. His recent despondency, not to say despair,
was gone in a moment. I never saw a man so thoroughly enjoy himself
amid the fragrance of lemon-peel and sugar, the odor of burning rum,
and the steam of boiling water, as Mr. Micawber did that afternoon. It
was wonderful to see his face shining at us out of a thin cloud of these
delicate fumes, as he stirred, and mixed, and tasted, and looked as if he
were making, instead of punch, a fortune for his family down to the lat-
est posterity . . .

The leg of mutton came up very red within, and very pale without—
besides having a foreign substance of a gritty nature sprinkled over it, as
if it had had a fall into the ashes of that remarkable kitchen fire-place.
But we were not in a condition to judge of this fact from the appearance
of the gravy, forasmuch as the "young gal" had dropped it all upon the

stairs—where it remained, by the bye, in a long train, until it was worn out. The pigeon pie was not bad, but it was a delusive pie; the crust being like a disappointing head, phrenologically speaking—full of lumps and bumps, with nothing particular underneath. In short, the banquet was such a failure that I should have been quite unhappy . . . if I had not been relieved by the great good-humor of my company, and by a bright suggestion from Mr. Micawber.

"My dear friend Copperfield," said Mr. Micawber, "accidents will occur in the best-regulated families; and in families not regulated by that pervading influence which sanctifies while it enhances the—a—I would say in short, by the influence of Woman, in the lofty character of Wife, they may be expected with confidence, and must be borne with philosophy. If you will allow me to take the liberty . . . I would put it to you, that this little misfortune may be easily repaired."

There was a gridiron in the pantry, on which my morning rasher of bacon was cooked. We had it in, in a twinkling, and immediately applied ourselves to carrying Mr. Micawber's idea into effect . . . Traddles cut the mutton into slices; Mr. Micawber (who could do anything of this sort to perfection) covered them with pepper, mustard, salt, and cayenne; I put them on the gridiron, turned them with a fork, and took them off, under Mr. Micawber's direction; and Mrs. Micawber heated, and continually stirred, some mushroom ketchup in a little saucepan. When we had slices enough done to begin upon, we fell-to, with our sleeves still tucked up at the wrists, more slices sputtering and blazing on the fire, and our attention divided between the mutton on our plates and the mutton then preparing.

What with the novelty of this cookery, the excellence of it, the bustle of it, the frequent starting up to look after it, the frequent sitting down to dispose of it as the crisp slices came off the gridiron hot and hot, the being so busy, so flushed with the fire, so amused, and in the midst of such a tempting noise and savor, we reduced the leg of mutton to the bone . . . I am satisfied that Mr. and Mrs. Micawber could not have enjoyed the feast more if they had sold a bed to provide it. Traddles laughed as heartily, almost the whole time, as he ate and worked. Indeed we all did, all at once; and I daresay there never was a greater success.

It is ironic that Micawber commends "Woman, in the lofty character of Wife" as the solution to David's difficulties where food preparation is concerned. David has been in love with the boss's daughter, and has the misfortune to win and wed her. Dora can't even *buy* food properly: "Everybody we had anything to do with seemed to cheat us. Our appearance in a shop was a signal for the damaged goods to be brought out immediately. If we bought a lobster, it was full of water. All our meat turned out to be tough, and there was hardly any crust to our loaves." What is amazing, then, is that David dares to bring home his same old school friend, Traddles, for dinner at all—and with only an afternoon's advance warning.

I could not have wished for a prettier little wife at the opposite end of the table, but I certainly could have wished, when we sat down, for a little more room . . .

There was another thing I could have wished, namely, that Jip [the dog] had never been encouraged to walk about the table-cloth during dinner . . .

However, as I knew how tender-hearted my dear Dora was, and how sensitive she would be to any slight upon her favourite, I hinted no objection. For similar reasons I made no allusion to the skirmishing plates upon the floor . . . I could not help wondering in my own mind, as I contemplated the boiled leg of mutton before me, previous to carving it, how it came to pass that our joints of meat were of such extraordinary shapes— and whether our butcher contracted for all the deformed sheep that came into the world; but I kept my reflections to myself.

"My love," I said to Dora, "what have you got in that dish?"

I could not imagine why Dora had been making tempting little faces at me, as if she wanted to kiss me.

"Oysters, dear," said Dora, timidly.

"Was that *your* thought?" said I, delighted . . .

"Ye-yes, Doady," said Dora, "and so I bought a beautiful little barrel of them, and the man said they were very good. But I—I am afraid there's something the matter with them. They don't seem right." Here Dora shook her head, and diamonds twinkled in her eyes.

"They are only opened in both shells," said I. "Take the top one off, my love."

"But it won't come off," said Dora, trying very hard, and looking very much distressed.

"Do you know, Copperfield," said Traddles, cheerfully examining the dish, "I think it is in consequence—they are capital oysters, but I *think* it is in consequence—of their never having been opened."

They never had been opened; and we had no oyster knives—and couldn't have used them if we had; so we looked at the oysters and ate the mutton. At least we ate as much of it as was done, and made up with capers. If I had permitted him, I am satisfied that Traddles would have made a perfect savage of himself, and eaten a plateful of raw meat, to express enjoyment of the repast; but I would hear of no such immolation on the altar of friendship; and we had a course of bacon instead; there happening, by good fortune, to be cold bacon in the larder.

Cooked, presumably. And by the domestic help, at that.

Mutton seems to be the most unfortunate victim in these passages, but also, through the magic of Micawber, the most fortunate. Reading that passage in which he salvages the raw-and-gray, cinder-covered flesh, turning it into the most mouth-watering dish, can actually be painful if you are hungry.

In this country, mutton is virtually unsold, and it's hard for me to believe that roasting would be the best method for cooking some tough old hunk of sinewy leg—braising or stewing would be more like it. But we don't have to worry about it: we have lamb. The closest approach I've had to Mr. Micawber's delicacy is a deboned leg of lamb as cooked by my friend Robin Beaty, a superb cook and domestic genius. Read the recipe through before trying this: the meat needs to be marinated, and a stock made from meat trimmings in advance.

Lamb à la Robin

marinade

  3 large cloves garlic, peeled
3–4 sprigs fresh thyme, or 1 tablespoon dried
  2 tablespoons chopped fresh rosemary, or 1 tablespoon dried
  1 tablespoon mustard seeds
  1 teaspoon freshly ground black pepper
  1 teaspoon ground cumin
  1 teaspoon fennel seeds
1½ tablespoons French mustard
  ¼ cup olive oil
  3 tablespoons freshly squeezed lemon juice
  1 teaspoon anchovy paste
  ½ cup red wine
  2 bay leaves

lamb

1 7–8 pound leg, boned, butterflied, and trimmed of fat (will be about 4½–5½ pounds of meat); save the trimmings and bones for the gravy

1. Chop together fresh herbs and garlic. Add remaining marinade ingredients except wine and bay leaves. Blend. (This can be done in a blender or food processor.)
2. Open meat out flat, fat side down. If necessary, cut lengthwise slashes to make the thickness more even. Spread about two thirds of the marinade over the surface of the meat and massage it into every crevice. Turn the meat over into a large oblong baking dish and pat it down snugly. Spread the rest of the marinade over the top. Drizzle red wine over lamb, tuck in bay leaves, and marinate overnight in refrigerator.
3. The next day, allow lamb to come to room temperature. Preheat broiler. Remove lamb from pan and reserve marinade. Lay lamb flat, fat side down, on an oiled broiling pan or rack. If necessary, run skewers crosswise through the meat to hold an even thickness and to secure any loose chunks of meat.
4. Place 4 to 5 inches under broiler, and broil 10 minutes per side.
5. Remove the meat from the broiler and reset oven for 375°. Allow lamb to sit at room temperature until oven is ready.*
6. Roast in upper third of 375° oven for 15 to 20 minutes, until lamb is rare. Remove lamb from oven and let rest 15 minutes while preparing the final steps of the gravy.

for gravy

Reserved bones and trimmings
Water
Reserved marinade
2 tablespoons butter, melted
4 tablespoons chopped fresh parsley

1. Make stock of reserved lamb bones and trimmings: place them snugly in pot with water to cover, and simmer, skimming the foam as needed, for at least 1 hour. Remove solids and boil stock down to 1 or 2 cups.

---

*This can be prepared in advance up to the final roasting (Step 6).

2. When ready to make the gravy, add reserved marinade to 1 cup of stock, bring to a simmer, and reduce by half.

3. Turn off the heat, and whisk in butter and parsley. Slice lamb thin. Add juices from slicing to the gravy and serve.

This should probably serve 6, but its succulence invites gluttony: it safely serves 4.

NOTE: The lamb may also be cooked on an outdoor barbecue. Grill instead of broiling, and cover with the hood for the roasting.

DINNER

Lamb à la Robin (recipe above)

Warm or cool salad of white beans, rice, parsley, and Vinaigrette*

*Butternut squash, steamed and puréed
(butter or sweetener optional)*

Zucchini, cut in ⅛-inch rounds and sautéed in oil until browned

*Figs, grapes, Explorateur cheese, and Butter Cookies
(recipe follows)*

*Recipe in *The Sweet Dove Died.*

Butter Cookies

The secret of these plain and simple cookies is to make them as thin as possible—as thin as you can make the dough without breaking it. Then they melt in the mouth, and are dangerously addictive.

½ pound sweet butter, softened
2 egg yolks
1 cup sugar
1 teaspoon vanilla
2½ cups flour
Pinch of salt

Preheat oven to 450°.

1. Mix all ingredients together with your hands. Try not to overwork the dough.
2. Make small balls, rolling between your palms to about ⅜ inch.
3. Flatten the balls using the side of one palm against the other palm. Place on cookie sheet and further flatten with the tines of a fork. Keep space between raw cookies.
4. Bake 5 minutes. Cookies should be *just* touched with brown at rims. They will rise and then settle just as they finish. Cookies may be decorated with sprinkles or sugar before baking.

Makes up to 9 or 10 dozen cookies.

THE DIARY OF A GOOD NEIGHBOUR

by Doris Lessing

(1 9 8 3)

A *top* editor at a popular and ambitious women's magazine in the late 1970s or early 80s has the following encounter one day at the drugstore:

I saw an old witch. I was staring at this old creature and thought, a witch. It was because I had spent all day on a feature, Stereotypes of Women, Then and Now. *Then* not exactly specified, late Victorian, the gracious lady, the mother of many, the invalid maiden aunt, the New Woman, missionary wife, and so on. I had about forty photographs and sketches to choose from. Among them, a witch, but I had discarded her. But here she was, beside me, in the chemist's. A tiny bent-over woman, with a nose nearly meeting her chin, in black heavy dusty clothes, and something not far off a bonnet. She saw me looking at her and thrust at me a prescription and said, "What is this? You get it for me." Fierce blue eyes, under grey craggy brows, but there was something wonderfully sweet in them.

I liked her, for some reason, from that moment. I took the paper and knew I was taking much more than that. "I will," I said. "But why? Isn't he being nice to you?" Joking: and she at once responded, shaking her old head vigorously.

"No, oh *he's* no good, I never know what *he's* saying."

He was the young chemist, and he stood, hands on the counter, alert, smiling: he knew her well, I could see.

"The prescription is for a sedative," I said.

She said, "I know *that*," and jabbed her fingers down on to the paper where I had spread it against my handbag. "But it's not aspirin, is it?"

I said, "It's something called Valium."

"That's what I thought. It's not a pain-killer, it's a stupefier," she said.

He laughed. "But it's not as bad as that," he said.

I said, "I've been taking it myself."

She said, "I said to the doctor, aspirin—that's what I asked for. But *they're* no good either, doctors."

All this fierce and trembling, with a sort of gaiety. Standing there, the three of us, we were laughing, and yet she was so very angry.

"Do you want me to sell you some aspirin, Mrs Fowler?"

He handed her the aspirin, and took her money, which she counted out slowly, coin by coin, from the depths of a great rusty bag. Then he took the money for my things—nail varnish, blusher, eye liner, eye shadow, lipstick, lip gloss, powder, mascara. The lot: I had run low of everything. She stood by watching, with a look I know now is so characteristic, a fierce pondering look that really wants to understand. Trying to grasp it all.

I adjusted my pace to hers and went out of the shop with her. On the pavement she did not look at me, but there was an appeal there. I walked beside her. It was hard to walk so slowly. Usually I fly along, but did not know it till then. She took one step, then paused, examined the pavement, then another step. I thought how I rushed along the pavements every day and had never seen Mrs Fowler, but she lived near me, and suddenly I looked up and down the streets and saw—old women. Old men too, but mostly old women. They walked slowly along. They stood in pairs or groups, talking. Or sat on the bench at the corner under the plane tree. I had not seen them. That was because I was afraid of being like them. I was afraid, walking along there beside her. It was the smell of her, a sweet, sour, dusty sort of smell. I saw the grime on her thin old neck, and on her hands.

The house had a broken parapet, broken and chipped steps. Without looking at me, because she wasn't going to ask, she went carefully down the old steps and stopped outside a door that did not fit and had been mended with a rough slat of wood nailed across it. Although this door wouldn't keep out a determined cat, she fumbled for a key, and at last found it, and peered for the keyhole, and opened the door. And I went in with her, my heart quite sick, and my stomach sick too because of the smell. Which was, that day, of over-boiled fish. It was a long dark passage we were in.

We walked along it to the "kitchen". I have never seen anything like it outside our Distress File, condemned houses and that sort of thing. It was an extension of the passage, with an old gas cooker, greasy and black,

an old white china sink, cracked and yellow with grease, a cold-water tap
wrapped around with old rags and dripping steadily. A rather nice old
wood table that had crockery standing on it, all "washed" but grimy. The
walls stained and damp. The whole place smelled, it smelled awful. . . .
She did not look at me while she set down bread, biscuits and cat food.
The clean lively colours of the grocery packages and the tins in that
awful place. She was ashamed, but wasn't going to apologize. She said
in an offhand but appealing way, "You go into my room, and find yourself a seat."

The room I went into had in it an old black iron stove that was showing a gleam of flames. Two unbelievably ancient ragged armchairs. Another nice old wood table with newspaper spread over it. A divan heaped
with clothes and bundles. And a yellow cat on the floor. It was all so dirty
and dingy and grim and awful. I thought of how all of us wrote about decor
and furniture and colours—how taste changed, how we all threw things
out and got bored with everything. And here was this kitchen, which if
we printed a photograph of it would get us donations by return from readers.

Mrs Fowler brought in an old brown teapot, and two rather pretty
old china cups and saucers. It was the hardest thing I ever did, to drink
out of the dirty cup.

It was the hardest thing I ever did, to drink out of the dirty cup. Tea is brac-
ing as well as soothing, it wakes you up, and Jane Somers, the impeccable
ladies' mag editor, is woken to a new life by that drink. It's her un-stupefier.
It is for her as if she has been half asleep until then, and living a life outside
of time. She has been under an enchantment, and doing "the hardest thing"
frees her. Through her friendship with the ancient crone, she becomes a part
of life, from first perceiving the other old ladies on the street ("I had not seen
them," her future) to becoming a writer: she turns the story of the old lady,
Maude Fowler's grim life—in which she was abandoned by a father and then
a husband, and her adored son stolen—into a romance novel. "Maudie would
have loved her life, as reconstructed by me."

In telling her diary the real story, Jane is uncompromising, and you get
everything, from the filth coating Maudie's crotch to Jane's fanatical attention towards her own gorgeous, custom-made, high-maintenance clothing. It
is a women's story in all the best senses, including that of giving full due to
what women traditionally care about: cleaning, clothing, food.

Most essentially, however, what Jane wakes up to is love, which she realizes she's never allowed herself to give before, neither to her mother or sister, nor to her not long dead and much-missed husband. She realizes that in

caring for this old lady she will be called neurotic, that her love will be written off as all kinds of other things, and as too extreme. Do you really have to drink from that *filthy* cup? In a Barbara Pym novel (not *Sweet Dove*), a character wonders, looking around at the unappealing parishioners in church, if, as a practicing Anglican, she really has to love all of them. In a story by Mary McCarthy, more famous for the silly reason of being sexually "shocking" than for being good, a woman goes to bed with an unappealing stranger and thinks, as he enjoys her body, that it is "the only real act of charity I have ever performed in my life."

The pressing question for Jane Somers, or her author, is how far you go for love; if it has limits, is it love? Is it love if you even ask? She is raising these questions in a world that takes it for granted that it is *crazy* to give unstintingly, crazy not to put yourself first. When she drinks her cup of tea and wakes up, Jane knows it is that way of thinking that is crazy.

M u c h of the Western world regards tea as consummately British, but it was not introduced into England until that small country began to be an empire, importing tea from Asia where it had been known, widely cultivated, and used for centuries. The reason there are tea caddies—lockable little chests—in early British novels is because tea was so precious a commodity at first that the few who could afford it kept it locked up like their silver spoons. Like coffee, it was looked upon as a potentially dangerous intoxicant when introduced to Europe. Like all intoxicants, it was immediately a great hit and in tremendous demand.

Coffee, more locally available here—from South America—became North America's drug of choice, so tea's association with the British has persisted. The symbolism of the Boston Tea Party was not entirely coincidental—to dump tea was to dump the British.

Since instant gratification and convenience are the American way, the teabag took over as the mode for brewing; since the United States became the dominant world power, you are now apt to get a cup of hot water with a teabag chastely beside it on the saucer even in a British restaurant. Maudie Fowler, being in her nineties and anything but convenient, naturally brews tea the old-fashioned way. However dirty that cup was, the tea was probably pretty good.

Brewed Tea

The standard formula for well-made tea is one teaspoonful of loose tea in the pot for each cup, plus one for the pot. That will make a strong pot of tea.

The water should start cold. Bring it to a full boil, let the bubbling stop, then pour the water over the leaves in the pot and give the mixture a stir. Let the tea steep in the pot for five minutes or so. A tea cozy over the pot will perfect the process.

The leaves will settle to the bottom for pouring, but the tea will be more homogeneous if you give it a second stir, then pour it through a strainer into the cups. In China, the steeped tea is often decanted into a thermos, where it will stay hot and not stew.

In England, honey is as traditional a sweetener for tea as sugar, along with a flavoring of either lemon (served in wedges on the side) or plain whole milk.

As a meal, "low tea" is an upper-class snack to tide you over until your elegantly late supper. "High tea" is lower class, and *is* supper or, more likely, dinner. "Cream tea" does not refer to what you put into the tea—it is *not done* to put cream in tea; it's what you slop onto the scones that are part of a cream tea. Tea can be anything from a cold roast or meat pie to those refined finger sandwiches, petit fours, and scones that hotels always serve—all good, but here's something different.

T E A

Honey and Orange Bread (recipe follows)

Apple and Cheese Bread (recipe follows)

Sesame Loaf (recipe follows)

Soft butter

Cream cheese

Apple wedges and grapes

Sharp cheddar, Gourmandaise cheese

Tea (recipe above), milk, lemon wedges, honey, sugar

Honey and Orange Bread

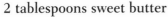

2 tablespoons sweet butter
1 cup honey
1 egg, beaten
1½ tablespoons grated orange zest
2½ cups flour
2½ teaspoons baking powder
½ teaspoon baking soda
½ teaspoon salt, or to taste
¾ cup orange juice
¾ cup chopped nuts

Preheat oven to 325°.

1. In a bowl large enough to hold all ingredients, cream butter with honey; add egg and orange rind when butter has become pale and fluffy.
2. Sift dry ingredients and add to butter mixture alternately with orange juice, stirring only until mixed. Add nuts just before final blending.
3. Turn into well-greased 9-inch loaf pan and bake 1 hour and 10 minutes.

Apple and Cheese Bread

2 cups flour
1 teaspoon baking powder
½ teaspoon baking soda
1 teaspoon salt or less
½ cup sweet butter
⅔ cup sugar
2 eggs
1 cup ground cored apple with juice and peel
½ cup grated cheddar or other sharp cheese
¼ cup walnuts, pecans, or other nuts

Preheat oven to 350°.

continued

1. Sift dry ingredients together.
2. In a bowl large enough to hold all the ingredients, cream butter; add sugar gradually until batter becomes pale and fluffy. Beat in eggs. Blend in apple, cheese, and nuts.
3. Add half of the dry mixture; blend just until moistened. Add remainder of the flour mixture in same manner.
4. Turn into well-greased 9-inch loaf pan, heaping the batter to the sides with a depression at the center. Bake 1 hour.

Sesame Loaf

3 cups flour
1 teaspoon salt or less
2½ teaspoons baking powder
½ cup toasted sesame seeds
¼ cup sweet butter
⅔ cup sugar
2 eggs
1 teaspoon lemon zest, grated
1½ cups milk
1 tablespoon untoasted sesame seeds

Preheat oven to 350°.

1. Sift flour, salt, and baking powder into a bowl large enough to hold all ingredients. Stir in the toasted sesame seeds.
2. Cream butter and sugar; beat in eggs. Stir in lemon rind and milk.
3. Add wet mixture to the dry. Cut and fold fifteen times; scrape down bowl. Cut and fold fifteen times again.
4. Turn mixture into well-greased, lightly floured 9-inch loaf pan. Sprinkle untoasted sesame seeds on top. Bake 1 hour 10 minutes.

BREAD OF
AFFLICTION

A LITTLE PRINCESS

by Frances Hodgson Burnett

(1 9 0 5)

N o v e l s would be no fun without troubles for the characters. *A Little Princess* grants all the luxuries of misery one could wish: it has the heroine's martyrdom in abundance, and also her virtue rewarded; it lets you revel in the starkest deprivation but also in beautiful clothes and sumptuousness—and all without your having to suffer the heroine's losing her very good manners, or having to move from your chair.

Sara Crewe comes at age seven to Miss Minchin's school for young ladies—a row house in London whose small number of pupils range in age from four to seventeen, and in intelligence from the mortally stupid Ermengarde to Sara, whose favorite occupation is to gulp down quantities of books and remember all of them. She also likes to make up and tell fantasies—to "suppose," as in "Suppose I were a princess."

She arrives at the school as its "show pupil," because her father is so indulgent and gives her things even the richest girls there don't have (ermine capes, dolls with custom-made wardrobes, a private sitting room—embellished with the skin of a tiger Captain Crewe shot in India, where he lives). So she is like a princess.

But four years later, Sara's "supposing" abilities are very much put to the test when her darling papa loses all his money on a diamond-mine venture and dies of worry and fever. Orphaned and indebted to the horrible Miss Minchin, Sara is relegated to the attic. Gone is the ermine, and even the doll's wardrobe. She becomes a ragged, starved errand girl. Treated as a servant even by the cook, Sara sustains herself by imagining that she is a princess in disguise. This makes it possible for her always to behave beautifully even as she is abused, and to be endlessly kind despite a lack of resources.

Sara's fall is anticipated in her friendship with Becky, the school's exploited scullery maid, to whom early on Sara smuggled cake until it occurred to her to buy meat-pies for the underfed slavey. "Oh, miss!" said Becky; "Them will be nice an' fillin'. It's fillin'ness that's best. Sponge-cake's a evingly thing, but it melts away like—if you understand, miss. These'll just *stay* in yer stummick." Becky also told the much-protected Sara that Becky had to eat these morsels quickly when she reached her attic room, " 'cos if I leaves the crumbs the rats come out to get 'em," adding matter-of-factly, "There mostly is rats an' mice in attics. You gets used to the noise they makes scuttling about."

When, after her fall, Sara is consigned to the attic room next door to Becky's, she copes with it by pretending that they are prisoners in the Bastille. So that when a rat does in due time appear there, she mentally addresses it: "Prisoners in the Bastille used to make friends with rats. Suppose I make friends with you." She names the rat Melchisedec and imagines a whole family in the wall to whom he brings the crumbs she supplies from her own meager meals. Her imagination is a novelist's and moralist's: it always lets her know what it is like to be in another's place, even a rat's. If it were not for her aristocratic sense of noblesse oblige, she would, in her drastically reduced circumstances, *be* a scrounging rat, entirely at the mercy of what others supply.

But like many children, she believes in the idea that, if she can sustain her imaginings, they will in some magic way come true. On a day when she is deeply worn from hunger and cold and her shoes are soaked, she tries to imagine herself out of discomfort:

> "Suppose I had dry clothes on," she thought. "Suppose I had good shoes and a long, thick coat and merino stockings and a whole umbrella. And suppose—suppose—just when I was near a baker's where they sold hot buns, I should find sixpence—which belonged to nobody. *Suppose*, if I did, I should go into the shop and buy six of the hottest buns and eat them all without stopping."

In the act of supposing this, she comes upon a fourpence in the mud. She is so scrupulous that she checks up and down the street for anyone who may have lost it. It happens that she *is* straight across from a baker's where fresh buns are just being set out—"large, plump, shiny buns, with currants in them."

> It almost made Sara feel faint for a few seconds—the shock, and the sight of the buns, and the delightful odours of warm bread floating up through the baker's cellar window.

On the doorstep of the shop, however, is a beggar girl, a girl who can't even remember the last time she has eaten, who has no place to live, and whose feet are not just wet but bare. Sara is famished, but she asks the proprietress of the shop if she has lost a fourpence before she buys the rolls, and points out that the woman has given her too many—six—though a "mist" rises in her eyes at the woman's kindness. When Sara goes back out, the beggar girl is

> still huddled up in the corner of the step. She looked frightful in her wet and dirty rags. She was staring straight before her with a stupid look of suffering, and Sara saw her suddenly draw the back of her roughened black hand across her eyes to rub away the tears which seemed to have surprised her by forcing their way from under the lids. She was muttering to herself.
>
> Sara opened the paper bag and took out one of the hot buns, which had already warmed her own cold hands a little.
>
> "See," she said, putting the bun in the ragged lap, "this is nice and hot. Eat it, and you will not feel so hungry."
>
> The child started and stared up at her, as if such sudden, amazing good luck almost frightened her; then she snatched up the bun and began to cram it into her mouth with great wolfish bites.
>
> "Oh, my! Oh, my!" Sara heard her say hoarsely, in wild delight. *"Oh, my!"*
>
> Sara took out three more buns and put them down.
>
> The sound in the hoarse, ravenous voice was awful.
>
> "She is hungrier than I am," she said to herself. "She's starving." But her hand trembled when she put down the fourth bun. "I'm not starving," she said—and she put down the fifth.
>
> The little ravening London savage was still snatching and devouring when she turned away. She was too ravenous to give thanks, even if she had ever been taught politeness—which she had not. She was only a poor little wild animal.

Like Melchisedec.

You could say that Sara's magic works. She imagined a sixpence and got a fourpence, which miraculously buys not four but six rolls. She loses her father but is found by his best friend and rescued, her fortune not just restored but expanded. She is able to make Becky her personal maid (after all, it is a princess, not a senator, that she imagines herself to be; it's a kind of moral democracy Sara practices, not the social kind). Rich, and grateful, she decides, like a princess, to "scatter largess." Going back to the bakery shop, she

finds the woman has taken in the beggar, mainly because of Sara's Christ-like example of sacrifice, honesty, and generosity.

Nearly a hundred years after this was written, a reader may be tempted to scoff at the convenience of these outcomes; imagination isn't magic, after all. But it has sustained millions, especially children, through their suffering; and by imagining a better world, some people have in reality been able to take the first step toward improving ours. The addition of such a book as this is one form of improvement.

This is a traditional recipe for currant buns. It will cost considerably more than sixpence just for the ingredients, but it yields thirty to forty buns.

Currant Buns

dough

1 cup milk
2 packages yeast
¼ cup lukewarm water
¼ cup butter, margarine, or vegetable oil
2 eggs, lightly beaten
5 cups sifted flour
½ cup sugar
1 teaspoon salt
1 cup dried currants
1 teaspoon allspice

glaze

1 egg, beaten alone or with dash of sugar and/or water

Preheat oven to 400° during second rising.

1. Scald milk with the butter and let cool to lukewarm.
2. Dissolve the yeast in water and let proof, if desired.
3. Mix the liquid ingredients together in one bowl and the dry in another, reserving 2 cups of the flour. Mix the liquid ingredients into the dry. Add remaining flour by working it in with your hands, kneading on floured board until dough is elastic. You may have a considerable amount of flour left over.
4. Compact dough into bowl, grease surface of dough, cover with a cloth, and let rise in warm place until doubled in bulk, about 1 hour.
5. Punch down. Divide dough and shape it into balls about 1½ inches in diameter. Place the balls 2 inches apart on greased cookie sheets. Flatten slightly. Cover and let rise in warm place until doubled, about ¾ hour.
6. Brush buns with glaze and bake 12 to 15 minutes, until golden brown.

Makes about 3 dozen buns.

THE MAYOR
OF CASTERBRIDGE
by Thomas Hardy
(1 8 9 5)

Though the title is far from suggesting it, the pivotal circumstances of this powerful tragedy turn on food: bread and brew. Not, in this case, the bread of affliction but afflicted bread. The brew, for its part, is archaic, a concoction called "furmity." Even a final wrenching twist of the story turns on food, or lack of it: a little bird starves to death.

It is tempting to give the entire first chapter in full, so shocking is it and so beautiful in its shadings. It is about a man selling his wife.

A couple are passing a country fair where "a few inferior animals, that could not otherwise be disposed of, and had been absolutely refused by the better class of traders," are being auctioned off. The couple stop because the man wants a drink. The wife steers him from the liquor concession to the slightly less prosperous tent under the words "Good Furmity Sold Hear." The beverage is described as "antiquated slop" (even then) made of "grain, flour, milk, raisins, and what not." The "haggish creature of about fifty" who is selling the stuff adds rum to the man's portion; the wife "but too sadly perceived that in strenuously steering off the rocks of the licensed liquor-tent she had only got into maelstrom depths here amongst the smugglers."

She doesn't know how particularly bad this drunk of her husband's will be. He begins to complain that if he had not married her at eighteen "like the fool that I was," and were not saddled with her and their babe in arms, he'd be "worth a thousand pound before I'd done o't." There's no reason to believe him—he's just a hay-trusser, a moderately skilled laborer—though his boast will prove to be true. Hearing that a damaged brood-mare is being sold, he complains that he doesn't see why a wife shouldn't be sold the same way. And proceeds to open up an auction on her to the layabouts assembled. At first they think it a joke, and even the wife, all too familiar with this idea of her husband's, is merely passive. But then

> "Mike, Mike," said she, "this is getting serious. O!—too serious!"
> "Will anybody buy her?" said the man.
> "I wish somebody would," said she firmly. "Her present owner is not at all to her liking!"

When no one bids, the man, Michael Henchard, raises the price a guinea. He does this five times before a sailor, who has merely popped his head into the tent to see what is going on, offers.

> But with the demand and response of real cash the jovial frivolity of the scene departed. A lurid colour seemed to fill the tent, and change the aspect of all therein. The mirth-wrinkles left the listeners' faces, and they waited with parting lips.
> "Now," said the woman, breaking the silence, so that her low dry voice sounded quite loud, "before you go further, Michael, listen to me. If you touch that money, I and this girl go with the man. Mind, it is a joke no longer."
> "A joke? Of course it is not a joke!" shouted her husband, his resentment rising at her suggestion. "I take the money: the sailor takes you. That's plain enough. It has been done elsewhere—and why not here?"

When we next encounter them, Susan, the wife, is in her forties and the baby, Elizabeth-Jane, is eighteen; and Henchard is a prosperous merchant of hay and grain, mayor of the booming market town of Casterbridge. If it were not for a blight upon the wheat, the next major acts of consequence would not occur.

The people of the town are near riot at having been sold bad wheat: "I have never before tasted such rough bread as has been made from Henchard's wheat lately. 'Tis that growed out that ye could a'most call it malt, and there's a list at bottom o' the loaf as thick as the sole of one's shoe," complains one. Henchard, in his effort to calm the mob, points out that "I was taken in in buying it as much as the bakers who bought it o' me." As in the earlier scene, a stranger appears, another kind of rescuer. Donald Farfrae, a Scotsman, shows Henchard how the wheat may be made wholesome again. Henchard is so impressed that he hires the man to manage his extensive business. Since everything in the book has consequences as exactly weighted as the elements in a physics experiment, it is inevitable that Donald will become mayor and

Henchard once again be reduced precisely to the level of wandering journeyman he was when in the furmity tent.

About that little bird. If the opening scene of a man selling his wife is sensational, and Henchard's subsequent prosperity satisfying despite one's reservations about him, the last chapters are so heart-wrenching—they so wring from Henchard's final situation every variation on remorse, regret, self-loathing, self-effacing devotion, and resignation—that it is only with pain that you force yourself to read on.

When given the opportunity, Henchard had tried to make up for his earlier abandonment of his wife and child by remarrying Susan and taking Elizabeth-Jane at eighteen as a "stepdaughter," after they come looking for him upon the death of the sailor, Newson. Donald Farfrae is interested in Elizabeth, but Henchard quarrels with him and forbids Elizabeth to see the man. Just before Henchard's financial decline, Susan falls ill and dies, leaving behind a letter to be read upon Elizabeth's marriage. But Henchard idly reads it immediately, and learns that the baby he abandoned died and that Elizabeth is really Newson's daughter. From that moment he cannot abide her, and regrets having forbidden her Farfrae.

At this point, a woman Henchard had inadvertently compromised in his "widowed" days, Lucette, turns up, ready to marry him simply to have her reputation restored. She hires Elizabeth as a companion, thinking to lure Henchard's visits this way. She is dismayed to learn that Henchard now dislikes his stepdaughter—but then, after encountering the sweet, handsome Farfrae, decides she doesn't mind.

It all ends badly. The silly Lucette marries Farfrae, and Elizabeth persists in loving her father (as she believes Henchard to be), living with him in poverty. Just as things begin to improve, the scandal of Henchard and Lucette's past indiscretions comes out; and then the further scandal of Henchard's treatment of Susan long before (the furmity woman reappears, as an accusing vagrant). The shock of the first scandal's public exposure kills the pregnant Lucette—which is fine, because then the good Elizabeth can have the terrific Donald. But this pleasure is shadowed—for the reader—when Newson, not dead at all, shows up. Henchard has finally learned to love Elizabeth as a daughter, and can't bear to lose her devotion. So he lies to prevent Elizabeth from knowing about Newson. When Elizabeth finds out anyway, she cannot forgive Henchard.

This is the part that is just unbearable—for me, at least. (And yes, the bird comes into it—I'm getting to that.) Michael Henchard—broken, hot-tempered but honest, clever, and hard-working, all too willing to face up to the mistakes he is all too liable to make, "one of his own worst accusers"—has finally learned how to love just when the person who has taught him gives up on him. This is the constantly repeated pattern of the book—you get what you want eventually, but only when it no longer matters.

And of course, this happens clear to the finish. Henchard banishes himself, taking off in his hay-trusser's gear, exactly as he had arrived twenty or more years before. He lives utterly to himself, utterly lonely, without ambition or energy—or self-pity; only self-reproach. But when he hears that the wedding of Elizabeth and Farfrae is to take place within a few days, he decides that he will dare just to show himself and offer a present. He can't offer much: he buys a goldfinch in a little cage, which is wrapped in newspaper for him.

When it comes to it, though, Elizabeth, "the once despised daughter who had mastered him and made his heart ache," reproaches him, and he humbly slinks off. A month later, she finds the "little ball of feathers" in the cage. Realizing what has happened, she goes off in search of her stepfather, remorseful in her own turn. It is not easy to find a journeyman laborer. In keeping with the plan of the book, however, she does find him, but too late: he has just died. A note pinned to his bed asks

> That Elizabeth-Jane Farfrae be not told of my death, or made to grieve on account of me.
>   & that I be not bury'd in consecrated ground.
>   & that no sexton be asked to toll the bell.
>   & that nobody is wished to see my dead body.
>   & that no murners walk behind me at my funeral.
>   & that no flours be planted on my grave.
>   & that no man remember me.

If for want of a nail a kingdom can be lost, here it is the kingdom of love that is lost, because of some antiquated slop and rough bread.

You have here essentially a recipe for furmity ("frumenty," according to the Oxford English Dictionary), if you want to try the antiquated slop. Eggnog would seem to be more likely to accord with contemporary tastes, though, in the way of sweet, milky, highly nutritional potentially alcoholic drinks. Especially this lighter version. Classic eggnogs that call for whipped cream and stiff-beaten egg whites are so thick that they need to be ingested with a spoon. This one is drinkable.

Eggnog

1 cup milk
1 whole egg, beaten, or 1 egg yolk
1 teaspoon sugar syrup*
Dash vanilla
Bourbon or rum to taste, optional
Whole nutmeg

1. Blend the first four ingredients in a blender or with a whisk or fork. Add liquor as desired.
2. Pour into a cup or glass and grate nutmeg over top.

Makes 1 serving; increase as needed.

NOTE: If you want this thicker, as the traditional Christmas treat or for company, cream may be substituted in whole or part for the milk. Even made with part-skim milk, this is great for kids as something simple and filling.

In these days of rampant salmonella, it may be safest to use eggs from free-ranging chickens, which, because of not being smashed on top of each other, breeding bacteria, are less likely to carry it.

HOLIDAY OPEN HOUSE

Eggnog (recipe above), mulled cider

Cut-Out Cookies (recipe follows)

Thumbprint Cookies (recipe follows)

Heaps of mandarin oranges or clementines

Broken-up slabs of dark semisweet chocolate and white chocolate

---

*Sugar syrup is what rum is made of, and is sold like rum, in rum bottles. If none is available, you can melt sugar in a pan and add it to the eggnog mixture.

Cut-Out Cookies

½ cup sweet butter
½ cup sugar
2 eggs
2½–2¾ cups flour
2 teaspoons baking powder
¼ teaspoon salt or less
1 teaspoon vanilla

Preheat oven to 375°.

1. Cream butter and sugar together in a bowl large enough to hold all the ingredients. Beat in eggs.
2. Sift together dry ingredients and add, with vanilla, to butter mixture. Blend. Squeeze into four balls and chill about 3 hours.
3. On surface dusted with flour, roll out dough to a ⅛ to ¼ inch thickness, or as desired. Press out shapes with cookie cutters. Place on greased cookie sheet. Decorate with sprinkles or colored sugar or, after baking and cooling, with icing, if desired. Bake 7 to 12 minutes.

Makes about 30 cookies.

Thos. Hardy

Thumbprint Cookies

The elusive, highly particular flavor of these cookies derives from the brown sugar.

½ cup sweet butter
¼ cup brown sugar
1 egg, separated
½ teaspoon vanilla
1 cup sifted flour
¼ teaspoon salt
¾ cup finely chopped walnuts, if desired
Fruit jelly

Preheat oven to 350°.

1. Cream butter and sugar together in a bowl large enough to hold all the ingredients. Beat in yolk; add vanilla.
2. Sift flour and salt together. Add to butter mixture, and blend. Chill.
3. Take dough by teaspoonsful and form balls. Beat egg white. Dip each ball into egg white, then roll in chopped nuts.
4. On greased cookie sheet, place 1 inch apart. Press thumb into center of each ball. Bake 12 to 15 minutes. Remove from sheet and cool. Fill thumbprint with jelly.

Makes about 18 cookies.

MOBY-DICK

by Herman Melville

(1 8 5 1)

You would think that in a book about the sea, the crucial food, if any, would be seafood. Such a supposition would be borne out by the early part of the story, the part that takes place on land, before Ishmael and his nobly unsavage friend Queequeg set foot aboard their whaling ship. Melville himself first went to sea in January, also from New Bedford, and this New Bedford section is as much about cold and hunger as anything else. When Ishmael happily and warmly shares a bed with Queequeg, Melville makes the wise observation that some little part of you must be chilly to appreciate the warmth, some discomfort must be felt before there can be comfort: "If you flatter yourself that you are all over comfortable, and have been so a long time, then you cannot be said to be comfortable any more." You must "lie like the one warm spark in the heart of an arctic crystal."

Likewise, as Leo Tolstoy has a peasant remark, hunger is the best cook. It is "quite late in the evening" when Ishmael and Queequeg, having journeyed on to Nantucket, go in search of supper in the strange town, in the chapter headed "Chowder." They find the hotel they have been searching for, the Try Pots. The proprietress says to them, "Clam or Cod?"

"What's that about Cods, ma'am?" said I, with much politeness.

"Clam or Cod?" she repeated.

"A clam for supper? a cold clam; is *that* what you mean, Mrs. Hussey?" says I; "but that's a rather cold and clammy reception in the winter time, ain't it, Mrs. Hussey?"

. . . Mrs. Hussey hurried towards an open door leading to the kitchen, and bawling out "clam for two," disappeared.

"Queequeg," said I, "do you think that we can make out a supper for us both on one clam?"

However, a warm savory steam from the kitchen served to belie the apparently cheerless prospect before us. But when that smoking chowder came in, the mystery was delightfully explained. Oh, sweet friends! hearken to me. It was made of small juicy clams, scarcely bigger than hazel nuts, mixed with pounded ship biscuit, and salted pork cut up into little flakes; the whole enriched with butter, and plentifully seasoned with pepper and salt. Our appetites being sharpened by the frosty voyage, and in particular, Queequeg seeing his favorite fishy food before him, and the chowder being surpassingly excellent, we despatched it with great expedition: when leaning back a moment and bethinking me of Mrs. Hussey's clam and cod announcement, I thought I would try a little experiment. Stepping to the kitchen door, I uttered the word "cod" with great emphasis, and resumed my seat. In a few moments the savory steam came forth again, but with a different flavor, and in good time a fine codchowder was placed before us.

We resumed business; and while plying our spoons in the bowl, thinks I to myself, I wonder now if this here has any effect on the head? What's that stultifying saying about chowder-headed people? "But look, Queequeg, ain't that a live eel in your bowl? Where's your harpoon?"

Fishiest of all fishy places was the Try Pots, which well deserved its name; for the pots there were always boiling chowders. Chowder for breakfast, and chowder for dinner, and chowder for supper, till you began to look for fish-bones coming through your clothes. The area before the house was paved with clam-shells. Mrs. Hussey wore a polished necklace of codfish vertebra; and Hosea Hussey had his account books bound in superior old shark-skin. There was a fishy flavor to the milk, too, which I could not at all account for, till one morning happening to take a stroll along the beach among some fishermen's boats, I saw Hosea's brindled cow feeding on fish remnants, and marching along the sand with each foot in a cod's decapitated head, looking very slip-shod, I assure ye.

The book is never so lighthearted again after this chapter, nor so cheerful about fish. On land, the marine motif can be a joke. At sea, it is a life-or-death proposition. They are on an expedition of carnage, killing the biggest fish of all. (Melville *insists* that whales are fish, not mammals, though he makes them human and more than human in his compassionate depiction. In a footnote, he even remarks on whale *milk*: "very sweet and rich . . . it might do well with strawberries.")

Queequeg is supposed to be the cannibal, but he is the most loving being in this nautical world. What comes to seem like real cannibalism is the slaughter of the whales. For someone to have seen it this way in the middle of the nineteenth century is extraordinary. "That mortal man should feed upon the creature that feeds his lamp, and, like Stubb [the second mate], eat him by his own light, as you may say; this seems so outlandish a thing that one must needs go a little into . . . it":

> . . . no doubt the first man that ever murdered an ox was regarded as a murderer; perhaps he was hung; and if he had been put on his trial by oxen, he certainly would have been; and he certainly deserved it if any murderer does. Go to the meat-market of a Saturday night and see the crowds of live bipeds staring up at the long rows of dead quadrupeds. Does not that sight take a tooth out of the cannibal's jaw? Cannibals? who is not a cannibal? I tell you it will be more tolerable for the Fejee that salted down a lean missionary in his cellar against a coming famine; it will be more tolerable for that provident Fejee, I say, in the day of judgment, than for thee, civilized and enlightened gourmand, who nailest geese to the ground and feastest on their bloated livers in thy paté-de-foie-gras.
>
> But Stubb, he eats the whale by its own light, does he? and that is adding insult to injury, is it? Look at your knife-handle, there, my civilized and enlightened gourmand dining off that roast beef, what is that handle made of?—what but the bones of the brother of the very ox you are eating? And what do you pick your teeth with, after devouring that fat goose? With a feather of the same fowl. And with what quill did the Secretary of the Society for the Suppression of Cruelty to Ganders formerly indite his circulars? It is only within the last month or two that that society passed a resolution to patronize nothing but steel pens.

Mostly, as it happens, the whales are not eaten by the men, but only rendered for their precious oil (like the awful marlin in *The Man Who Loved Children,* see page 159); "tried" for oil. The rare taste of whale that is attempted is described as being "something as I should conceive a royal cutlet from the thigh of Louis le Gros might have tasted, supposing him to have been killed the first day after the venison season, and that particular venison season contemporary with an unusually fine vintage of the vineyards of Champagne." What a wonderful way of saying rich, gamy, and high.

The real demon of this story is not the dangerous killer whale Moby Dick but, as virtually everyone knows, the ship's captain, Ahab. Moby Dick took one of Ahab's legs, and Ahab has made it his personal quest to take the unkillable whale's life. Ahab is far less human than his quarry. Only too late does Ahab discover his humanity, too late to recover it, as he speaks to first mate Starbuck about the bread of affliction he has gratuitously swallowed:

> When I think of this life I have led; the desolation of solitude it has been; the masoned, walled-town of a Captain's exclusiveness, which admits but small entrance to any sympathy from the green country without—oh, weariness! heaviness! Guinea-coast slavery of solitary command!—when I think of all this; only half-suspected, not so keenly known to me before—and how for forty years I have fed upon dry salted fare—fit emblem of the dry nourishment of my soul!—when the poorest landsman has had fresh fruit to his daily hand, and broken the world's fresh bread, to my mouldy crusts—away, whole oceans away, from that young girl-wife I wedded past fifty, and sailed for Cape Horn the next day, leaving but one dent in my marriage pillow—wife? wife?—rather a widow with her husband alive! Aye, I widowed that poor girl when I married her, Starbuck; and then, the madness, the frenzy, the boiling blood and the smoking brow, with which, for a thousand lowerings old Ahab has furiously, foamingly chased his prey—more a demon than a man!—aye, aye! what a forty years' fool—fool—old fool, has old Ahab been!

As Melville comments in a chapter on provisioning the ship: "if you can get nothing better out of the world, get a good dinner out of it, at least."

Dry Salted Fare (Crackers)

6¾ cups unbleached or whole-wheat flour
6 tablespoons sugar
2 tablespoons baking powder
1 tablespoon (or more) salt plus extra salt for sprinkling
¾ cup vegetable oil
¾ cup milk
3 eggs, lightly beaten
Extra flour for kneading

Preheat oven to 350°.

1. Combine dry ingredients.
2. In separate bowl, beat together oil, milk, and eggs. Add dry ingredients slowly to wet, mixing only enough to make consistency workable; mix until smooth, in food processor or with dough attachment of electric beater, or use fingers. It may be easiest to divide ingredients into two batches, making sure not to add too much flour to either one. If dough gets too stiff, add more milk.
3. Turn dough onto lightly floured board. Knead until smooth and elastic. Separate into small balls, 1 inch or less, and flatten between palms or with a rolling pin to make as thin as possible.
4. Place on lightly greased baking sheets. Sprinkle with salt. Bake about 15 minutes, until golden. Remove from sheet and cool.

Makes about 50 crackers.

NOTE: Extra or unused dough may be molded into a ball, tightly wrapped in foil or plastic, and frozen.

For flavor, the following may be added in the first step: up to 1½ cups finely chopped pistachios or cashews; or up to 4½ teaspoons ground cumin, pepper, or grated lemon zest; or grated sharp cheese such as cheddar or Parmesan, ¼ to ½ cup or to taste.

The following is a recipe passed along to me thirty years ago by a Vermonter who baked bread every week, and did not use cookbooks. The instructions, transcribed in pencilled printing when I was ten, carefully preserve locutions like "Add till *right* consistency." For those who couldn't be there, I am providing more conventional measures.

The World's Fresh Bread

2 cups milk
3 tablespoons honey
1 tablespoon salt
3 tablespoons vegetable oil
1 cup lukewarm water
2 packages yeast
1 teaspoon sugar
3 cups sifted unbleached white flour
2–3 cups whole-wheat flour
2–3 further cups sifted unbleached white flour

Preheat oven to 350° after final rising.

1. Combine milk, honey, salt, and oil; scald.
2. Combine water, yeast, and sugar; let work.
3. When milk mixture has cooled to lukewarm (just above body temperature), mix with yeast blend.
4. Add liquid ingredients to 5 cups white and whole-wheat flour and mix. Keep adding flour until dough is firm enough to turn onto lightly floured board. Continue adding flour while kneading until firm, nonsticky dough is achieved.
5. Place in greased bowl, grease exposed surface of dough, cover with cloth, and allow to rise in warm spot until doubled in bulk.
6. Punch down. Cut in half (see Note). Knead into two loaves. Grease two 9 × 5 × 3-inch loaf pans. Place dough in pans and grease exposed surface. Let rise until again doubled in bulk.
7. Bake 50 minutes. Finished loaves should make hollow sound when tapped on bottom with knuckles or wooden spoon.

NOTE: Depending on how much flour has been added, the dough may be too much for two loaves (if, for instance, there is enough to fill two loaf pans *before* rising). If so, divide it into three loaf portions and proceed as above, using three pans.

STARVED LOVE

ETHAN FROME

by Edith Wharton

(1 9 1 1)

E*than Frome* is about a man who is starving. He lives in the Massachusetts mountain town of Starkfield, on a failing farm, surrounded by snow, with a woman as chilly as the landscape. He gets beans to eat, "cold mince-pie in a battered pie-dish," milk, and tea, but he is deprived of human contact in every significant way: one of the smart ones who was going to get away, he had to leave school to care for his dying father's farm, and was left with a mad mother who squandered all its little wealth. She would not speak, leaving him so desperate for contact that he married her nurse, Zeena—Zenobia—who would. But once having gotten him, she becomes like his mother: she barely speaks, and, seven years older than Ethan, at thirty-five she is like an old woman. "Sickness and trouble: that's what Ethan's had his plate full up with, ever since the very first helping."

Further, having no one else to nurse, Zeena becomes her own best patient, throwing Ethan's scant resources away on patent medicines and visits to an ever-widening circle of doctors for imaginary complaints.

But eventually, like the illness of his mother, this brings Ethan solace in the form of Zeena's cousin Mattie, the orphan daughter of an embezzling father, who is moved in to do the housework for which Zeena is supposedly too weak. She is pretty—and she speaks to him. Of course, they fall in love.

Though they speak, they are inarticulate about what matters, and their love goes unstated. Merely to have dinner alone together by the fireside is their height of bliss, on an evening Zeena is away to see a doctor. The very ordinariness of the event—"fresh doughnuts, stewed blueberries"—mimics marriage and therefore charms Ethan. But Mattie has also included in this plain main course "his favorite pickles in a dish of gay red glass."

Their tryst-like, quasi-clandestine, pseudo-marital dinner is eyed covetously by the cat, who becomes an incarnation of Zeena's presiding spirit, like a witch's familiar:

> The cat, unnoticed, had crept up on muffled paws from Zeena's seat to the table, and was stealthily elongating its body in the direction of the milk-jug, which stood between Ethan and Mattie. The two leaned forward at the same moment and their hands met on the handle of the jug. Mattie's hand was underneath, and Ethan kept his clasped on it a moment longer than was necessary. The cat, profiting by this unusual demonstration, tried to effect an unnoticed retreat, and in doing so backed into the pickle-dish, which fell to the floor with a crash . . .
>
> It seemed to him as if the shattered fragments of their evening lay there.

Before this catastrophe, Zeena had already been scheming to get rid of Mattie, not out of jealousy but because "the one pleasure left her was to inflict pain on him," Ethan. But when she discovers her loss, all hell breaks loose. When Zeena finally speaks, Ethan could well wish she wouldn't:

> "I went to get those powders I'd put away in father's old spectacle-case, top of the china-closet, where I keep the things I set store by, so's folks sha'n't meddle with them—" Her voice broke, and two small tears hung on her lashless lids and ran slowly down her cheeks. "It takes the stepladder to get at the top shelf, and I put Aunt Philura Maple's pickle-dish up there o' purpose when we was married, and it's never been down since, 'cept for the spring cleaning, and then I always lifted it with my own hands, so's 't shouldn't get broke." She laid the fragments reverently on the table . . .
>
> "You wanted to make the supper-table pretty; and you waited till my back was turned, and took the thing I set most store by of anything I've got, and wouldn't never use it, not even when the minister come to dinner, or Aunt Martha Pierce come over from Bettsbridge—" Zeena paused with a gasp, as if terrified by her own evocation of the sacrilege. "You're a bad girl, Mattie Silver, and I always known it. It's the way your father begun, and I was warned of it when I took you, and I tried to keep my things where you couldn't get at 'em—and now you've took from me the one I cared for most of all—" She broke off in a short spasm of sobs that passed and left her more than ever like a shape of stone.

Ethan thinks of running off with Mattie, but it occurs to neither of them just to refuse to go along with Zeena's plan of sending Mattie away, such is

Zeena's malevolent power. All they come up with, instead, is a suicide pact—to crash-sled into a tree. When they carry it out, Mattie is crippled, Ethan thrown clear. They end up indeed like the glass dish, irreparably shattered. They are consigned to a lifetime of emotional starvation and physical misery while Zeena fattens on her dominion over them.

Well! So much for pickles; let's stick to that meat pie, served hot. And not in a "battered pie-dish," either. Actually, it tastes good at room temperature too.

This is a mince-meat pie in the sense that it uses ground beef (though almost any other cut-up cooked meat will do).

Beef Tart

base

¾ pound ground beef
1 small onion, chopped
2 tablespoons butter
1 stalk celery, chopped
¼ pound ham, cut into ¼-inch pieces
1 egg, beaten
½ cup grated Swiss cheese
¼ cup grated Parmesan cheese
¼ cup chopped fresh parsley
1 teaspoon dried thyme
Salt and freshly ground black pepper to taste

topping

2 eggs, beaten
2 cups mashed winter squash: acorn, butternut, cheese
    pumpkin, or Hubbard (cooked)
½ cup cooked rice
⅔ cup cream
1 tablespoon melted butter
Salt and freshly ground black pepper to taste
¼ cup grated Parmesan cheese

continued

crust

> 1 10-inch or deep-dish pastry shell, baked at 425° for 8 minutes
> and cooled

Preheat oven to 350°.

1. Brown beef (if uncooked). Place in bowl to drain off liquid.
2. Sauté onion in butter; add celery and cook until wilted. Add ham and
   cook a minute or two more. Add to beef.
3. Add remaining ingredients of base and mix.
4. In a separate bowl, mix all ingredients of topping except Parmesan.
5. Press meat mixture into bottom of pastry shell. Cover with topping.
   Sprinkle with Parmesan. Bake 15 minutes, then turn heat down to 325°
   and bake for 20 to 30 minutes, or until crust is browned and the filling
   heated through.

Serves 3 to 5 for lunch or dinner.

LUNCH

Beef Tart (recipe above)

Tomatoes Vinaigrette*

The World's Fresh Bread** and butter

Berries and/or cherries

*Recipe in *The Sweet Dove Died.*
**Recipe in *Moby-Dick.*

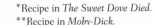

JANE EYRE
by Charlotte Brontë
(1 8 4 7)

Many people think of *Jane Eyre* as the love story of a poor but spunky governess who wins the crusty heart of her rich employer, with the mad wife in the attic the obstacle a good plot needs, as if the story were no more than a forebear of Barbara Cartland, et al. (The madwoman in the attic has become a rallying point of feminist literary criticism.) But the first part of *Jane Eyre* is about Jane's awful life as an orphan cousin in her wealthy aunt's household, and then as the inmate of a charity school to which the vile aunt sends her, Lowood; just as the last chunk of the novel lets Jane finally reunite with the good side of her family: if she had met them as a child, none of the bad stuff would ever have happened—and there would be no novel.

As usual, we sadomasochistic readers love for our heroines to suffer extravagantly and unjustly. In deference to their nobility, we may tolerate their forgiveness of injustices, but we certainly don't forget the suffering and we don't want them to either. And none of us is really good enough to be happy if they start in with forgiving before they have been fully rewarded in all areas where they were previously deprived.

Jane is, for a child of the educated classes, pretty thoroughly deprived. She is first of all deprived of parents—of love. She is deprived of money, which would have given her power at least to demand a simulacrum of love. And most of all, her various deprivations are concretely expressed as hunger. She is fed very badly as a child, and remains puny—with a rather chilly personality to go with the underdeveloped body. From the outset, hers is a story of too little, too late.

The opening scenes are of violence and cruelty. Ten-year-old Jane is beaten by her big fourteen-year-old male cousin, and then locked in the room where her uncle died, which is believed haunted. There she faints and falls into a fever. This alarms everyone, including the nursery maid who has been none too kind to her, and who in fear tries to make it up to the harrowed little girl:

> Bessie had been down into the kitchen, and she brought up with her a tart on a certain brightly painted china plate, whose bird of paradise, nestling in a wreath of convolvuli and rosebuds, had been wont to stir in me a most enthusiastic sense of admiration; and which plate I had petitioned to be allowed to take in my hand in order to examine it more closely, but had always hitherto been deemed unworthy of such a privilege. This precious vessel was now placed on my knee, and I was cordially invited to eat the circlet of delicate pastry upon it. Vain favour! coming, like most other favours long deferred and often wished for, too late! I could not eat the tart: and the plumage of the bird, the tints of the flowers, seemed strangely faded: I put both plate and tart away.

How is a tart and a pretty plate to make up for gross mistreatment? Too little, too late.

The maid, Bessie, is still not thoroughly chastened, however. She agrees with Aunt Reed's personal maid that it would be easier to care for the little girl if she were not "such a little toad"; it *is* easy to "doat" on the spoiled little monster girl cousin, with her "Long curls and her blue eyes, and such a sweet colour . . . just as if she were painted!"

The aunt's maid segues straight into

> "Bessie, I could fancy a Welsh rabbit for supper."
> "So could I—with a roast onion. Come, we'll go down." They went.

This is about as close to comedy as *Jane Eyre* comes—just the sheer incongruity of these two gratifying themselves while being so ostentatiously bitchy. They have good fellowship and access to food and warmth, valuable and not easily come by commodities in pre-modern Europe. Jane has none of these. She isn't pretty, she isn't rich, and she isn't theirs. Bessie tells her she is "less than a servant, for you do nothing for your keep."

Though most readers are likely to remember Lowood, the school, as a much greater horror, to Jane it has the virtues of companionship and the possibilities of rewards for good behavior. It is pretty awful, though, and replete with starvation. Jane's first morning there, which no one has taken the trouble to soften even by offering her information about the school's routines, is

unforgettable. She washes in freezing water, before dawn, in a basin shared
by six girls, then sits to Bible readings for an hour, by which time

day had fully dawned. The indefatigable bell now sounded for the fourth
time: the classes were marshalled and marched into another room to
breakfast: how glad I was to behold a prospect of getting something to
eat! I was now nearly sick from inanition, having taken so little the day
before.

The refectory was a great, low-ceiled, gloomy room; on two long tables smoked basins of something hot, which however, to my dismay, sent
forth an odour far from inviting. I saw a universal manifestation of dis-
content when the fumes of the repast met the nostrils of those destined
to swallow it; from the van of the procession, the tall girls of the first class,
rose the whispered words:—

"Disgusting! The porridge is burnt again!"

"Silence!" ejaculated a voice . . . A long grace was said and a hymn
sung; then a servant brought in some tea for the teachers, and the meal
began.

Ravenous, and now very faint, I devoured a spoonful or two of my
portion without thinking of its taste; but the first edge of hunger blunted,
I perceived I had got in hand a nauseous mess: burnt porridge is almost
as bad as rotten potatoes; famine itself soon sickens over it. The spoons
were moved slowly: I saw each girl taste her food and try to swallow it;
but in most cases the effort was soon relinquished. Breakfast was over,
and none had breakfasted. Thanks being returned for what we had not
got, and a second hymn chanted, the refectory was evacuated for the
school-room. I was one of the last to go out, and in passing the tables, I
saw one teacher take a basin of the porridge and taste it; she looked at
the others; all their countenances expressed displeasure, and one of
them, the stout one, whispered:—

"Abominable stuff! How shameful!"

In the brief interval that follows, during which talking is permitted, "The
whole conversation ran on the breakfast, which one and all abused roundly."

But here is where a good angel intervenes, Miss Temple, the pretty, young
superintending teacher.

"You had this morning a breakfast which you could not eat; you must
be hungry:—I have ordered that a lunch of bread and cheese shall be
served to all . . . It is to be done on my responsibility."

The bread and cheese was presently brought in and distributed, to the high delight and refreshment of the whole school.

Still, Miss Temple's powers are limited. The school's official superintendent is Mr. Brocklehurst, a classic Victorian villain, all selfishness and sadism disguised by mealy-mouthed piety. So after Miss Temple's nice bread and cheese, Jane is subjected to the following two meals:

The odour which now filled the refectory was scarcely more appetising than that which had regaled our nostrils at breakfast: the dinner was served in two huge tin-plated vessels, whence rose a strong steam redolent of rancid fat. I found the mess to consist of indifferent potatoes and strange shreds of rusty meat, mixed and cooked together. Of this preparation a tolerably abundant plateful was apportioned to each pupil. I ate what I could, and wondered within myself whether every day's fare would be like this . . .

Soon after five P.M. we had another meal, consisting of a small mug of coffee, and half a slice of brown bread. I devoured my bread and drank my coffee with relish; but I should have been glad of as much more—I was still hungry. Half an hour's recreation succeeded, then study; then the glass of water and the piece of oat-cake, prayers, and bed. Such was my first day at Lowood.

Looking back, the narrating Jane comments on the routine:

. . . the scanty supply of food was distressing: with the keen appetites of growing children, we had scarcely sufficient to keep alive a delicate invalid. From this deficiency of nourishment resulted an abuse, which pressed hardly on the younger pupils: whenever the famished great girls had an opportunity, they would coax or menace the little ones out of their portion. Many a time I have shared between two claimants the precious morsel of brown bread distributed at tea-time; and after relinquishing to a third, half the contents of my mug of coffee, I have swallowed the remainder with an accompaniment of secret tears, forced from me by the exigency of hunger.

On Sundays,

A little solace came at tea-time, in the shape of a double ration of bread—a whole, instead of a half, slice—with the delicious addition of a thin scrape of butter: it was the hebdomadal treat to which we all looked forward from Sabbath to Sabbath. I generally contrived to reserve a moi-

ety of this bounteous repast for myself; but the remainder I was invari-
ably obliged to part with.

Then, Mr. Brocklehurst makes an appearance:

"I find, in settling accounts with the housekeeper, that a lunch, consisting of bread and cheese, has twice been served out to the girls during the
past fortnight. How is this? I look over the regulations, and I find no such
meal as lunch mentioned. Who introduced this innovation? and by what
authority? . . . You are aware that my plan in bringing up these girls is,
not to accustom them to habits of luxury and indulgence, but to render
them hardy, patient, self-denying. Should any little accidental disap-
pointment of the appetite occur, such as the spoiling of a meal, the
under or the over dressing of a dish, the incident ought not to be neu-
tralised by replacing with something more delicate the comfort lost, thus
pampering the body and obviating the aim of this institution; it ought to
be improved to the spiritual edification of the pupils, by encouraging them
to evince fortitude under the temporary privation . . . you may indeed feed
their vile bodies, but you little think how you starve their immortal souls!"

Jane does indeed grow up hardy, patient, and self-denying. But it is said
that, in order to grow up not totally cold, all that is needed is for at least one
person to have shown you love. Miss Temple provides a temperate sort of
love, but it is love all the same, and expressed, not surprisingly, in hot tea,
toast, and seed cake. When Miss Temple can't get extra bread and butter from
the cook for the private tea she gives Jane and her friend Helen, Jane char-
acterizes the cook as "a woman after Mr. Brocklehurst's own heart, made up
of equal parts of whalebone and iron."

An epidemic of typhus sweeps over the school. For Jane, however—having become hardy—it is not an unmitigated disaster.

Semi-starvation and neglected colds had predisposed most of the
pupils to receive infection: forty-five out of the eighty girls lay ill at one
time . . . The few who continued well were allowed almost unlimited li-
cence . . .

I, and the rest who continued well, enjoyed fully the beauties of the
scene and season: they let us ramble in the wood, like gipsies, from
morning till night; we did what we liked, went where we liked: we lived
better too . . . the cross housekeeper was gone . . . her successor . . . unused to the ways of her new abode, provided with comparative liberality.
Besides, there were fewer to feed: the sick could eat little; our breakfast-
basins were better filled: when there was no time to prepare a regular din-

ner, which often happened, she would give us a large piece of cold pie, or a thick slice of bread and cheese, and this we carried away with us to the wood, where we each chose the spot we liked best, and dined sumptuously . . .

Inquiry was made into the origin of the scourge, and by degrees various facts came out which excited public indignation in a high degree. The unhealthy nature of the site; the quantity and quality of the children's food; the brackish, fetid water used in its preparation; the pupils' wretched clothing and accommodations: all these things were discovered; and the discovery produced a result mortifying to Mr. Brocklehurst, but beneficial to the institution.

When Jane finally leaves Lowood after eight years to become the governess to Mr. Rochester's illegitimate daughter, she is at pains in her narration to smooth over all the ill-treatment with which she has rankled the reader's soul, emphasizing her good education, and having the old nursery maid, Bessie, pay a fond farewell visit. Though, again, in the popular conception Jane in the end goes off dancing the fandango, a Victorian Cinderella, the fact is that she has been quite realistically warped by her childhood deprivations: she marries a blinded man and won't wear pretty dresses. But, presumably, she does not force on herself burnt porridge.

And I will not force it on my readers. If you want to try burnt porridge, just cook it over too high a heat, don't stir it, and leave it on the stove too long.

But you're not a product of deprivation, I hope; *you* can still enjoy that bright plate, that delicate pastry. Still, a fancy pastry, or even Welsh rarebit, would seem out of keeping with plain Jane. For me, both sensual delight and hardiness are to be found in a good granola, and I have never had granola to equal this from a hippie recipe passed along to me in 1969. It is so delicious that I cannot resist eating it hot, like cookies, straight from the oven, picking out the juiciest stuck-together clumps with my fingers.

Granola

4 cups rolled oats
1 cup unsweetened dry shredded coconut
½ cup hulled sesame seeds
1 cup walnuts and/or cashews, pecans, sunflower seeds
½ cup wheat germ (optional)
½ teaspoon salt (optional)
½ cup honey or maple syrup
½ cup vegetable oil

Preheat oven to 350°.

1. Mix dry ingredients in a large bowl.
2. Add honey and stir until it is well integrated.
3. Add oil and stir again.
4. Spread on flat pans to a depth of no more than 1½ inches. Cook 15 to 20 minutes. As mixture begins to brown and be fragrant, gently turn it in pan at 5-minute intervals until it is golden (or darker if you like it crunchier—or burnt!).
5. Set pans away from heat to cool. To prevent hardening into one solid crust, break the mixture up as it cools by turning it a last time.

NOTE: Granola will keep indefinitely. Serve with milk, fruit, yogurt, or eat it plain. Over baked apples and cream, it's dessert.

EATING
THE SOCIAL
INDEX

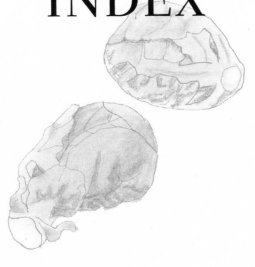

COLD COMFORT FARM
by Stella Gibbons
(1 9 3 2)

Food is not absolutely central to *Cold Comfort Farm*, but as you might expect of a book with "comfort" in the title, it has, at least, an important role. The book was written as a parody of some popular fiction of the time, maybe most notably, or most obviously, that of Erskine Caldwell and D.H. Lawrence. But it supersedes its aim; it is unnecessary to have read (or dislike) those writers to enjoy this as a silly comic romp, despite its digs at all things bohemian or Romantic. It can be read as a defense of classicism (which is also, sadly, in its very English way, here a defense of class).

When upper-class Flora Poste is orphaned at twenty without a proper inheritance, she chooses to live with some unmet relatives who have been mysterious about a "wrong" done to her father and "rights" she is owed. It is not because she thinks she'll get some material benefit out of this, however, that she goes, but because she looks forward to straightening her relatives out—so stereotypically uncouth and mysterious do they sound. Upon her arrival, everything is just as unpromising as she could wish. The nearest village is called Howling, and the train doesn't even go there. She is greeted in an appropriately uncivilized way. But by behaving as if all were normal, insisting, in airily polite bromides, on her comforts, she soon manages to find herself "beside a smoky fire in her room, pensively eating two boiled eggs." Her room is magnificent. You know Flora is going to make out and have her way in all things.

But first she is confronted by a dirty, barren farm (which an American would be more likely to call an estate, with its hundreds-of-years-old "farm-house" containing uncounted bedrooms and extra sitting rooms) and numbers of hulking, lunky, dialect-muttering Starkadder cousins with names like

Micah and Urk. In short order, she gets Amos, the putative head of the estate, who likes to preach to the "Quivering Brethren," to go off as a traveling evangelist "in one of they Ford vans"; gets gorgeous ladykiller cousin Seth, who lives only for the "talkies," into Hollywood movies; teaches an overly fertile, unmarried serving girl about birth control; and eventually takes the wood-sprite-ish cousin Elfine in hand to make her boring enough for the local scion of the gentry to marry. In short, she's an Emma who has to suffer no comeuppance whatsoever. (In fact, her cousin Reuben, a competent farmer, is so grateful to her for getting rid of Amos—which enables Reuben to run the farm—that he proposes.)

Early on, Flora is concerned that "there might be a difficulty about her food while she was at Cold Comfort." All anyone seems to eat is porridge. It is not only "coarse," but when it falls on the floor, it is ladled back into the pot. She finds bread at the farm, presumably home-baked, "not bad," however; and those eggs, from free-ranging chickens in the yard, must be delicious even if, *horreur*, she has to cook them herself. She tries dinner at the local pub, the Condem'd Man: she is forced to the labor of buying her own steak from the butcher, but the pub folk cook it well and serve it with apple tart and vegetables. Finally she catches sight of a real solution to her food dilemma when she sees the breakfast tray left outside the door of the as-yet-unseen tyrannical Aunt Ada Doom, transported by an actual servant, Mrs. Beetle:

> Flora watched Mrs Beetle stagger upstairs with a tray laden with sausages, marmalade, porridge, a kipper, a fat black pot of strong tea, and what Flora caustically thought of as half a loaf . . .

Among the dinners provided for Aunt Ada Doom are, on "Monday, pork; Tuesday, beef; Wednesday, toad-in-the-hole; Thursday, mutton; Friday, veal; Saturday, curry; Sunday, cutlets." Flora, naturally, is clever enough to get in on this gravy train, and takes her meals alone, for the most part, in bed or in an otherwise unused sitting room, by a fire, while the rest eat their porridge in the kitchen:

> Meals at the farm were eaten in silence. If anyone spoke at all during the indigestible twenty minutes which served them for dinner or supper, it was to pose some awkward questions which, when answered, led to a blazing row . . . On the whole, Flora liked it better when they were silent, though it did rather give her the feeling that she was acting in one of the less cheerful German highbrow films.

Very nearly the apex of Flora's ascendency over the Doom-Starkadder clan is her arranging the wedding of Elfine to the nob Dick Hawk-Monitor at which "syllabubs, ice-pudding, caviare sandwiches, crab patties, trifle, and champagne" are served to the peasantry, and "cider, cold home-cured ham, home-made bread, and salads made from local fruit" are set out for the gentry. To complete this picture of the upward-aspiring tastes of the lower classes in contrast with a taste for "simplicity" among the loaded, the County gentry table is decorated with "cottage flowers" and the peasant one with blooms imported from a Covent Garden florist.

But it is the series of meals leading up to this that will complete Flora's triumph. Flora has decided to beard the much-feared Aunt Ada Doom in her den (which Aunt Ada only ever leaves twice a year). Explaining nothing, but getting the Starkadders quite excited, Flora tells those in the kitchen,

> "I am going to take her lunch up to Aunt Ada . . . If I have not come down by three o'clock, Mrs Beetle, will you kindly bring up some lemonade. At half past four you may bring up tea and some of the currant cake Phoebe made last week. If I am not down by seven o'clock, please bring up a tray with supper for two, and we will have hot milk and biscuits at ten. Now good-bye, all of you. I beg of you not to worry. All will be well." . . .
>
> That was the last that anyone heard or saw of her for nearly nine hours . . . Mrs Beetle wondered a dozen times if she should not just run up with a few sandwiches and some cocoa at nine, in order to see whether there were any developments to be observed. But Reuben said no, she was not to; she had been told to take up hot milk at ten o'clock, and hot milk at ten she should take; he would not have Flora's instructions disobeyed by the tiniest detail. So she stayed where she was.
>
> They all got very cosy, sitting round the open door in the lingering twilight; and presently Mrs Beetle made them all some barley water, flavoured with lemon, and they sat sipping it comfortably, for their throats were quite sore with talking and wondering what on earth Flora could be saying to Aunt Ada Doom . . .

Flora comes down at ten-fifteen, exhausted, but explains nothing. In the morning she even further mystifies and amazes everyone by saying that Aunt Ada "doesn't want anything for breakfast except a Hell's Angel":

> Mrs Beetle stared, while Flora tossed an egg, two ounces of brandy, a teaspoonful of cream and some chips of ice in a jam-jar, and everybody else was very interested, too.

The final amazement is that Aunt Ada comes downstairs for the wedding feast, "dressed from head to foot in the smartest flying kit of black leather," and announces that she is going to the Hôtel Miramar in Paris.

> On this, confusion broke forth . . . The Starkadders were so flabbergasted, so knocked clean out of the perpendicular by the bosom-shattering stupendosity of the event, that nothing but a good deal of food could persuade them to shut their mouths.

Flora never does "get her rights," or even learn what they are. Nor does she find out what "wrong" was done her father. All she learns is that it concerned a goat.

There is so much food in Cold Comfort that one could base an entire cookbook on it. But most of the food is elementary—boiled eggs, steak, and the everlasting porridge. The most poetic-sounding of the dishes, however, are alluring: syllabub, a Hell's Angel (for which the story provides a fully detailed recipe), and toad-in-the-hole, which sounds as wonderfully disgusting as life at Cold Comfort itself before Flora whips it into shape. It is certainly no health dish, and would definitely go on the gentry's table at the wedding feast, being just as plain and homely as a, well, toad. The toads here are sausages; their burrows are in Yorkshire pudding. Yorkshire pudding, if you've never had it, is less like a pudding than like a wickedly large popover. With a salad or broccoli rabe and sweet squash on the side, this is a comforting chilly-weather meal. Lucky old fat Aunt Ada.

Toad-in-the-Hole

English bangers are the traditional sausages to use in this, but I like pork breakfast sausages. Use whatever sausages you like best.

    1 cup sifted flour
    ½ teaspoon salt
    1 cup milk
    2 eggs, lightly beaten
    1 pound sausage

gravy

2 cups beef broth
2 tablespoons butter
2 tablespoons flour

Preheat oven to 450°.

1. Mix 1 cup flour and salt. In a separate bowl, beat together milk and eggs. Continuing to beat, add the flour mixture; beat until mixture is frothy. Cover loosely and set aside for ½ hour, away from heat.
2. Prick the sausages and brown them on the stove or under the broiler to render the fat.
3. Heat an 11 × 7 inch baking pan and spread ¼ cup of the sausage drippings to coat. Pour in batter and top with sausages.
4. Bake for 10 minutes. Reduce the oven temperature to 350° and bake 15 to 20 minutes more, until pudding is puffed up, golden, and crusty.
5. Melt butter in saucepan over medium heat while broth simmers in separate pot. Add flour to butter and whisk together over heat for a few minutes. Slowly pour in broth, whisking, until the gravy achieves desired thickness. You may wish not to use all the broth. Remove from heat.
6. Cut finished pudding into serving portions, and serve with gravy.

Serves 4 to 6.

NOTE: It is important to the success of the recipe to heat the baking pan before adding the drippings and batter. Do not omit this step.

DINNER

Toad-in-the-Hole (recipe above)

Broccoli rabe sautéed with garlic and steamed in its own juices

Baked Acorn Squash, with butter and maple syrup (recipe follows)

Baked Acorn Squash

    1 acorn squash
2–4 tablespoons butter
2–4 tablespoons maple syrup

Preheat oven to 350°.

1. Split squash lengthwise and scrape out seeds and fibers. Wipe exposed edges with butter.
2. Drop 1 tablespoon butter and 1 to 2 tablespoons maple syrup into each half.
3. Bake 45 minutes to 1 hour. Squash should yield easily to fork and be slightly browned.

Serves 2.

NOTE: To accompany dishes that don't include pork, you can substitute ½ slice raw bacon and 1 teaspoon brown sugar for the butter and maple syrup in each half squash.

ALICE ADAMS

by Booth Tarkington

(1 9 2 1)

*I*f Booth Tarkington is remembered at all, fifty or so years after his death, it is for his two novels that were turned into movies, *Alice Adams* and *The Magnificent Ambersons*, both of which also won him Pulitzer Prizes. The books themselves are to be found now only in secondhand shops and the kind of libraries that hold on to volumes no one's taken out in years. However, the books must have something: I read *Alice Adams* when I was about ten—my parents' and grandparents' bookshelves were like that kind of library—and it made an excruciating impression that did not fade. And most excruciating was the dinner scene that forms the climax of the story.

It comes late in this short novel, as the culmination of Alice's courtship by a wealthy young man, when Alice's mother decides that respectability requires he formally meet the rest of the family. Alice has met the man at a ball given by one of the leading social lights of their industrial Midwestern town. Like a character out of Louisa May Alcott, Alice wears a gown that's been remade, but unlike those forthright heroines, Alice has done this to disguise the gown's familiarity. Her whole life, as it turns out, is one of dissimulation, of trying to pretend she's on an equal footing with the upper-crust set she went to school with before they abandoned her for eastern colleges. Alice's father is a clerk.

Tarkington takes a punishing delight in humiliating and mortifying his heroine, so that the experience of reading the book is one of sympathetically cringing and flinching—and of what could be called sociological fascination.

For the fatal dinner in honor of the classy boyfriend, Mr. Russell, Mrs. Adams hires a "day worker" to cook and has the woman procure a maid to wait table. An elaborate meal is planned:

"I thought we'd have little sandwiches brought into the 'living room' before dinner . . . We can make them look very dainty, on a tray . . . Then, after the soup, Malena says she can make sweetbread patés with mushrooms: and for the meat course we'll have larded fillet . . . We'll have peas with the fillet, and potato balls and Brussels sprouts. Brussels sprouts are fashionable now, they told me at market. Then will come the chicken salad, and after that the ice-cream—she's going to make an angel-food cake to go with it—and then coffee and crackers and a new kind of cheese I got at Worlig's, he says is very fine."

In fact, hors d'oeuvres are such a novelty that when the sullen serving woman offers one to Adams, he says, "What you want o' me?" He is even more dismayed when the caviar that is in them reaches his tongue, never before having had the opportunity to acquire this taste, and finally takes the chance of dropping the "damp and plastic sandwich" into the fireplace as the others file in to the even more dreadful ordeal to come.

> Alice, glancing back over her shoulder, was the only one who saw him . . . seeing that he looked at her entreatingly, as if he wanted to explain that he was doing the best he could, she smiled upon him sunnily, and began to chatter to Russell again.

It's a badly staged performance, underfunded and underrehearsed, in which even the audience must play a part: that of a delighted audience.

On top of the social discomfort, this giant, heavy dinner—for which Adams has been forced into hot evening clothes that hang on a frame wasted from a stroke—is taking place on a summer day of "heat like an affliction." The dinner also presents the intersection of the romantic plot, in all its unromance, with another.

Russell has just heard that Adams is opening a factory of his own, to manufacture glue. The glue formula is actually owned by the boss Adams left—one of the town's very biggest wheels, J. A. Lamb: Russell's relative. Alice doesn't know what Russell's heard, nor does she believe her father has done anything wrong, though he complains at home of how he cannot stop smelling the glue, a very Raskolnikov of glue works. When he complains of the odor before the dinner, Alice says,

> "How absurd you are about your old glue smell, papa!" . . .
> "I didn't mean glue," he informed her. "I mean cabbage. Is that fashionable now, to have cabbage when there's company for dinner?"

It's the smell of the Brussels sprouts, against which they have futilely opened every window. Even without knowing what Russell has heard, Alice knows this dinner is fatal, but has lied to herself at least as much as she's lied to him. Despite her tremendous uneasiness, part of her believes that she can keep up the lie by arranging the few roses they can afford on the table in a pretentious manner. Throughout the dinner, her mortifying chatter is non-stop.

> . . . the sight of hot soup might have discouraged a less determined gaiety. Moreover, there were details as unpropitious as the heat: the expiring roses expressed not beauty but pathos, and what faint odour they exhaled was no rival to the lusty emanations of the Brussels sprouts . . .
>
> The small room, suffocated with the odour of boiled sprouts, grew hotter and hotter as more and more food appeared, slowly borne in, between deathly long waits, by the resentful, loud-breathing Gertrude. And while Alice still sought Russell's glance, and read the look upon his face a dozen different ways, fearing all of them; and while the straggling little flowers died upon the stained cloth, she felt her heart grow as heavy as the food, and wondered that it did not die like the roses.

Mr. Adams is essentially decent and unpretending, but has been pushed into his drastic action with the glue formula by the ambitious Mrs. Adams. But as if that act of dishonesty were not enough to highlight the unfortunate Alice's little hypocrisies—the smell of the sprouts and glue is finally the very stench of guilt—the end of the awful dinner is graced by the delivery of news that Alice's brother has embezzled from J. A. Lamb and run off. You would think that was absolutely the end, but Alice's worst mortification is to accept the realities of her class and learn to be a stenographer.

Just as Alice constantly worries about what Russell may hear of her— that they have no money, that she isn't really accepted by the society set— Adams worries what J. A. Lamb is saying about Adams's defection. The gluey heat, the smelly meal, the glue of society—it's as if *Pride and Prejudice* had been boiled down to its ugliest elements.

There is nothing subversive about *Alice Adams*. Tarkington seems to believe that strivers *should* not succeed. He has the ability to see society clearly—and yet not to mind. He can describe how the heat affects each according to their status:

> Dripping negro ditch-diggers whooped with satires praising hell and hot weather, as the tossing shovels flickered up to the street level, where sluggish male pedestrians carried coats upon hot arms, and fanned themselves

with straw hats, or, remaining covered, wore soaked handkerchiefs between scalp and straw. Clerks drooped in silent, big department stores; stenographers in offices kept as close to electric fans as the intervening bulk of their employers would let them . . .

Yet despite the clarity of vision that distinguishes how life worsens in precise proportion to one's descent in the social hierarchy—employers get the cooling breeze, employees don't—Tarkington makes the black servants into vaudeville darkie caricatures and refers to one as a "hired African immune" (immune to the heat). Tarkington's nervous validation of all the values that finally rewarded him has earned him his present obscurity, morally if not aesthetically. Even as he identifies with ditch-diggers, he sides with the bosses.

W h a t the Adamses didn't know about Brussels sprouts would probably fill a book, but I am not going to write it. They undoubtedly boiled those sprouts until they were good and dead, and then left them hanging around till dinnertime on heat until they were putrid. Nor is summer the ideal time to harvest the little cabbages, except maybe the very baby ones (under an inch in diameter) developing at the bottom of the stalk, and only if you have your own garden. Even then, you'd probably want to serve them at room temperature in a vinaigrette. Otherwise, Brussels sprouts are at their peak after the first frost, which gives them a nutlike flavor unlike any other vegetable, and makes them sweeter than at any other time. These cannot be found in supermarkets, but at farmers' markets and produce stands, where they may be sold on the stalk.

But even the most humdrum sprouts in waxy cardboard pints from the grocery can be wonderful if they are fresh and do not get overcooked. Dropped into good, simmering broth until just tender, then served in the broth, sprinkled with grated Parmesan, they are delicious, and even dietetic. Quartering the sprouts before cooking will ensure that they cook evenly, the inside tender without being mushy, the outside slightly crisp. (Slice each sprout in half from crown through stem, and cut each half again to make four wedges.) The briefly boiled, steamed, or microwaved sprouts can also be sautéed with cut-up bacon; with chopped onions or shallots in butter or oil; or, classically, with butter and cooked shelled chestnuts.

Try the following recipe on people who state categorically that they detest Brussels sprouts. They will change their minds—hence the name Conversion Sprouts.

Conversion Sprouts

¾–1 pound Brussels sprouts, cleaned and quartered
3–5 tablespoons butter or oil
½ cup chopped onion, sautéed
½–1 cup ricotta cheese
½–1 cup grated Swiss or Parmesan cheese
Salt and freshly ground black pepper to taste
¼ pound Genoa salami, cut into ¼-inch strips, or cooked loose
　　sausage meat
egg (optional)

Preheat oven to 300° or slightly higher.

1. Mix all the ingredients together and turn into lightly greased soufflé dish
   or casserole. Sprinkle with additional cheese if desired.
2. Bake 20 to 30 minutes, until thoroughly heated and egg has set (the mixture will still be soft rather than firm).

Serves 4.

NOTE: The proportions above may be varied depending on how much vegetable you want in relation to cheese/protein.

DINNER

Roast chicken

Conversion Sprouts (recipe above)

Orzo browned in oil with pine nuts

*Salad of red and yellow sweet pepper strips dotted with goat cheese
on bed of greens, in Vinaigrette* with dash of orange juice*

Lemon Squares (recipe follows)

*Recipe in *The Sweet Dove Died.*

Lemon Squares

crust

> 1 cup butter
> ½ cup confectioners' sugar
> 2 cups flour

filling

> 4 eggs
> 2 cups sugar
> 6 tablespoons flour
> 6 tablespoons lemon juice
> 6 tablespoons grated lemon zest
> Confectioners' sugar for dusting

Preheat oven to 350°.

1. Combine crust ingredients in food processor or with fingers. Press into a 10 × 15 inch baking pan (or equivalent), with sides high enough to hold at least one inch of filling. Keep thickness as even as possible. Bake for 20 minutes.
2. Lightly beat eggs. Blend in sugar, flour, lemon juice, and zest. Spread over baked crust. Bake 25 minutes.
3. Cool. Cut into squares as small as 1 × 1 inch—the flavor is intense. Remove from pan. The squares may be frozen at this point for later use, or dusted with confectioners' sugar for serving within the next several days. (Serve at room temperature, but store in refrigerator.)

*Makes up to 100 squares, depending on size,
and serves between 4 and 20.*

MARJORIE
MORNINGSTAR
by Herman Wouk
(1 9 5 5)

arjorie Morgenstern is Alice Adams as a Jew. Like Alice, she's a social climber; like Alice, the fate she most wants to avoid is the one staring her in the face: working as a stenographer (only, in this case, for her father, who has a millinery-supply business). Like Alice, Marjorie wants to be an actress and, if she marries, will not consider the more ordinary eligible prospects, but only the most stellar, hard-to-get man. Like *Alice Adams*, *Marjorie Morningstar* is set between world wars but, unlike the earlier book, it is written in a very different time—which it reflects far more faithfully than it does the period it means to depict.

It almost goes without saying that, like Alice, Marjorie is exceptionally pretty. What is different from Alice, however, is that this is virtually her only personal attribute. As punitive as Tarkington is toward his heroine, he's a sweetheart compared to Mr. Wouk.

Each man has written his story as a kind of object lesson, a story about an Everygirl. (It wouldn't be a woman; for them, there are girls, and there are matrons.) Wouk gives a playwright character the last word on Marjorie: he says she is boring "by any technical standard." That's Wouk's little joke: the novel sold any number of copies, and a watered-down version was made into a movie starring Natalie Wood and Gene Kelly. One wonders, what is that technical standard he's talking about? Because what makes one cringe while reading the book, and indeed, what makes it compelling—despite the most careless, sloppy prose, attitudinizing, flagrant contrivance, and unjustified grandiosity of conception—is that the Pulitzer Prize–winning author's condescending tone suggests throughout that he is on to some celestial standard the rest of us can only guess at, and by which a Marjorie—any middle-class young woman with aspirations—is not just ordinary, but *unforgivably* ordinary: too ordinary to achieve significantly, and too ordinary not to want to.

So—what does this have to do with food? Marjorie's parents are immigrants, and have been Orthodox Jews until the move to Central Park West with which the story begins. Marjorie grew up not eating pork or shellfish, though she does not otherwise observe the laws of keeping kosher. As she pushes toward worldly status, her reluctance to eat shrimp cocktail or bacon is mocked by the more sophisticated Jews she's trying to impress: where brunch at Tavern on the Green includes bacon, brunch at the Morgensterns' features smoked fish. To Wouk this is not merely a realistically observed detail; he is a writer of his time, a period when people used the word "symbol" unself-consciously in reference to fiction. As it turns out, smoked fish is what good girls have. What bad girls have is sex.

The big question in the story is, Will Marjorie have sex? In this, the book is less like *Alice Adams* than *Pamela.* By the time Marjorie willingly eats lobster (even if she calls it a "big red bug") you know she's pretty close to doing the deed; and when she hardly notices that she's eating pork, she's practically porking. When, in the last chapter, she's not only avoiding such foods but actually keeping kosher, she is married and all transgression is behind her.

As to whether transgression and aspiration might be the same thing, and a good thing, Wouk is startlingly clear: yes, they may be—for a man. He puts his views into the mouth of Marjorie's great love, the insufferable Noel Airman (originally Saul Ehrmann), who harangues Marjorie on the subject, saying she gets the idea from popular media that women are supposed to have independent identities and accomplish things (this is supposed to be the 1930s). He scoffs that a woman should do what she is "built" to do—sexually please a man, raise "his" children, and keep him content to do his work. Marjorie's most spirited response, at any point, is to call Noel a "cruel hound," and otherwise say "Yes, dear" at every possible opportunity. She is never allowed any consciousness, or a single idea.

More amusing is the parallel way in which food and sex are described. When Marjorie is taken to the highest-priced restaurant in New York (which apparently is supposed to mean that it's also the best restaurant), the food is "unbelievable"—a typically evocative Wouk description—so good that Marjorie feels it as "humiliating" to her uneducated palate. (It is the only instance known to me of humiliation by deliciousness.)

These same key words come into play in Marjorie's surrender to Noel and sex. At first she finds being naked with him fairly delicious, if unexciting. But then it becomes too unfamiliar and strenuous—so unfamiliar as to do more than merely startle and surprise, yielding "pain, incredible humiliation, shock, shock, and it was over."

If you want a trustworthy account of defloration in the 1930s, read *The Group.* Beyond that, I don't know that I can come up with a recipe for any food that is properly humiliating; but I was mortified once when I served the following lobster dish for a New Year's Eve gathering and ruined it by dumping this (unbelievably, incredibly) delicious sauce on so much pasta that you could barely taste it. I felt humiliated, but I don't think my guests did.

One advantage to serving lobster this way: it does not look like a big red bug.

Linguini with Lobster Sauce

Th i s recipe has three parts. The first two, cooking the lobster and making a lobster bisque, can be done in advance—and probably should be if you don't want to be daunted by the many steps. Some fish markets sell cooked lobster and prepared lobster bisque. These are unlikely to be as good as making your own—often the bisque is too salty, and the lobster overcooked and untender—but it can be a useful shortcut. The final assembly may have steamed asparagus tips, or peeled asparagus cut into short bits, or peas, added to it, to taste.

for cooking the lobster

 2 1½-pound or 3 1-pound lobsters
 1 onion, chopped
 1 carrot, chopped
 1 stalk celery, chopped
 1 slice lemon, quartered
 8–10 sprigs fresh parsley
 2 bay leaves
 4 sprigs fresh thyme, or pinch dried
10–12 cracked black peppercorns
 2 cups white wine
 1 tablespoon salt

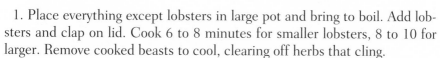

1. Place everything except lobsters in large pot and bring to boil. Add lobsters and clap on lid. Cook 6 to 8 minutes for smaller lobsters, 8 to 10 for larger. Remove cooked beasts to cool, clearing off herbs that cling.
2. Allow broth in pot to cook down. Strain 1 cup of cooking broth to use in bisque.

3. Shell lobster, reserving meat, coral, and shells. Be sure to remove gravelly stomach sac. Cut meat into small pieces for final assembly.

for making the bisque

Lobster shells, smashed to slightly flatten
3 tablespoons olive oil
1 tablespoon cognac or grappa
1 carrot, finely chopped
1 onion, finely chopped
1 stalk celery, finely chopped
½ sweet red pepper, finely chopped
¼ cup white wine
Dash cayenne pepper, or to taste
½ cup or more reserved lobster broth
Reserved lobster coral

1. Sauté shells in oil for 2 minutes. Add cognac and reduce heat. Add vegetables, wine, cayenne, and ½ cup broth. If shells stand above liquid, add water and a bit more broth to cover. Simmer 30 minutes.
2. Strain and cook down to about 2 cups. Add coral; whisk.

for the sauce and final assembly

1 carrot, finely chopped
1 onion, finely chopped
1 stalk celery, finely chopped
3 tablespoons butter
1 bay leaf
Salt and freshly ground black pepper to taste
2 sprigs fresh thyme, whole
2 sprigs fresh thyme, minced
6–8 sprigs Italian parsley, minced
16–18 sprigs fresh chervil, minced (reserve 2–3 sprigs for garnish)
1 cup heavy cream (not ultrapasteurized)
1 cup lobster bisque
Reserved lobster meat
1–2 teaspoons cognac or grappa
1¼ pounds fresh thin linguini

1. Cook chopped vegetables in butter over medium-low heat with bay leaf, salt, pepper, and whole thyme sprigs 5 to 7 minutes. Remove herbs.

2. Cook heavy cream down for a minute or two; add the bisque and stir.
3. Add minced fresh herbs, cooked vegetables with butter, cut-up lobster meat, and the cognac. Keep warm, but do not allow to simmer or boil.
4. Cook noodles and drain. Toss noodles in sauce and taste for seasoning. Garnish with remaining chervil.

Serves 4 to 6.

COMPANY DINNER

Hors D'Oeuvres: Salmon Loaf,* Dry Salted Fare,** cherry tomatoes, baguette cut into thin rounds

Linguini with Lobster Sauce (recipe above)

Green beans in butter and fresh minced tarragon, served next to

White string beans, same sauce

Garlic Egg Custard with Shiitake (recipe follows)

Hazelnut-chocolate Daquoise with toasted almonds

(from a bakery)

Garlic Egg Custard with Shiitake

This dish is indecently, if not humiliatingly, delicious.

for the custard

12 good-sized cloves garlic
1 pint heavy cream (not ultrapasteurized)
4 egg yolks
Salt to taste
White pepper to taste
Grated Parmesan, Gruyère, or other cheese (optional)

Preheat oven to 270°.

*Recipe in *The Beggar Maid.*
**Recipe in *Moby-Dick.*

1. Peel garlic and remove bitter stem end. Simmer in cream over low heat until cream is reduced by about a third and garlic is soft. Mash garlic in the cream. Add yolks, salt, pepper, and cheese.

2. Butter shallow baking dish or custard cups and pour in the custard mixture to a height of no more than 2 inches. Sprinkle with additional Parmesan if desired. If using custard cups, place in a bath of hot water halfway up the sides. Bake up to 40 minutes, till moderately firm. If you want a browned surface, run custard under broiler to finish.

for the mushroom sauce

2–3 tablespoons sweet butter
8 shiitake, sliced
8 other mushrooms, sliced
3 scallions (including greens), minced
2 cups chicken stock
Salt and white pepper to taste
3 tablespoons minced chives
⅔ cup toasted broken walnuts

1. Melt enough butter to cover surface of a saucepan. Sauté mushrooms with scallions. Add stock, raise heat, and let liquid reduce by a third or so. Add salt and pepper. Remove from heat.

2. Just before serving, stir in 1 tablespoon of butter to melt, and add chives and walnuts. Reheat if necessary. Sauce may be served in a boat like gravy, poured over the whole custard, or spooned onto individual portions before serving.

Serves 3 to 6.

THE COOK
DID IT,
or KILLING WITH
KINDNESS

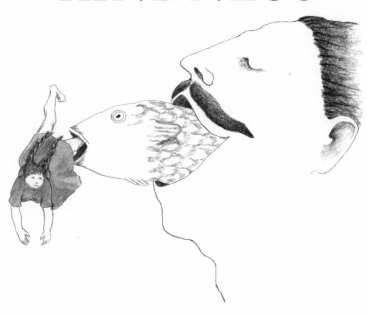

"LAMB TO THE SLAUGHTER"

by Roald Dahl

(1 9 4 9)

In this very famous story, dramatized for TV by Alfred Hitchcock, food becomes the blunt instrument of a violent murder. The story is extremely simple: A British policeman, Patrick Maloney, tells his six-months-pregnant wife, Mary, that he wants to leave her for another woman. The wife bashes him over the head with a frozen leg of lamb. She shoves it in the oven at high heat and rushes off to buy vegetables, neatly providing herself with an alibi. "Discovering" the dead husband when she comes home, she finds she doesn't have to feign sorrow and tears, and calls his precinct to say he's been murdered. Her husband's professional pals spend hours looking for a "big spanner" or "heavy metal vase": "Get the weapon, and you've got the man." When the lamb is cooked, she insists they take a break and eat it.

> "Here you all are, and good friends of dear Patrick's too, and helping to catch the man who killed him. You must be terribly hungry by now because it's long past your supper time, and I know Patrick would never forgive me, God bless his soul, if I allowed you to remain in his house without offering you decent hospitality."

She sits on in the living room with the body while they eat, listening to them, "their voices thick and sloppy because their mouths were full of meat." They're saying things like

> "That's the hell of a big club the guy must've used to hit poor Patrick . . . The doc says his skull was smashed all to pieces just like from a sledge-hammer."
> "That's why it ought to be easy to find."

. . . "Personally, I think it's right here on the premises."

"Probably right under our very noses . . ."

And in the other room, Mary Maloney began to giggle.

As does the reader, meanwhile wondering if, after this last line of the story, some detective is going to figure it out. Did the husband say to a friend, "I'm having it out with her tonight. It may be a hell of a scene"? We don't know. (We don't even really know what he tells his wife; it's so trite a situation, the author can leave it smoothly implied.)

Smooth though it is, the story is written with a child's delighted sense of creepiness, and is purest comedy. Even the opening, with that proper wife sewing, waiting to serve her husband: "She loved to luxuriate in the presence of this man, and to feel—almost as a sunbather feels the sun—that warm male glow that came out of him to her when they were alone together."

Of course, only a young child or an unfaithful man would find devoted love a big joke, but the tone is persuasively mocking. The fact that her devotion turns instantly to murderousness is also like something out of a childhood world, as is the joke made of cooking a proper, cheering, wholesome dinner, complete with two veg. Much of the story is little more than a description of its preparation—the kind of potatoes to accompany the lamb, a can of peas, and the store's cheesecake for dessert.

Equally childish is the idea that a leg of lamb, shoved into the oven at high heat without any further preparation, will taste like anything but hot greasy rubber. In Dahl's case, the food of love does not translate into love of food.

R o a s t leg of lamb that is not greasy and rubbery takes a certain amount of care—and as much garlic as possible.

Roast Leg of Lamb

   1 6-pound leg of lamb
1–3 cloves garlic, slivered
   2 tablespoons melted butter
   2 tablespoons vegetable oil
   1 large carrot, coarsely sliced
   1 large onion, coarsely sliced
3–6 cloves garlic, unpeeled
   1 teaspoon salt
¼ teaspoon freshly ground black pepper
   1 cup brown stock (lamb or beef)

Preheat oven to 450°.

1. Trim every vestige of fat from meat, without breaking encasing filament. Towel meat dry. Making small incisions, insert garlic slivers along shank and throughout.
2. Combine butter and oil and brush or spread with your fingers over lamb. Place meat on rack in snug roasting pan in upper third of oven to sear for 15 to 20 minutes, basting every 4 or 5 minutes.
3. Remove from oven. Reset temperature to 350°. Scatter onion, carrot, and unpeeled garlic in roasting pan. Return to oven, but set at middle level, and roast for 1 to 1¼ hours. Insert carving fork deeply into meat to test for doneness: the juice should run pink but not red. (If juice is yellow, the roast is probably overdone, unless you like it gray, hard, and dry.)
4. Transfer roast to hot platter and sprinkle it with salt and pepper. Do not attempt to carve it for at least 20 or 30 minutes.
5. Pour pan drippings into a fat-separator or small vessel; allow juices to settle while fat rises to top. Skim off fat. Return the defatted juices to the roasting pan and add stock. Over medium heat, scrape up the hardened drippings and mash the vegetables while the liquid bubbles. Strain into sauceboat.
6. Carve meat with sharp, preferably curved, carving knife, cutting from shank end toward thigh, on a horizontal, as thinly as possible. Serve on heated plates, to prevent congealing.

DINNER

Roast Leg of Lamb (recipe above)

Flageolet beans heated in butter

*Roast tomatoes stuffed with lemon-moistened bulgur, mint, and
pine nuts*

*Salad of Bibb lettuce, endive, clementine or mandarin orange
sections, red pepper slivers, and Vinaigrette**

Cheesecake, of course—store-bought

*Recipe in *The Sweet Dove Died.*

THE MAN WHO LOVED CHILDREN

by Christina Stead

(1 9 4 0)

The Man Who Loved Children is the scathing title of a book about a man who, in the guise of playing with and enlightening his many offspring, commits every kind of injustice against them. What is most hateful about him is his blithe unawareness of his crimes—a cheerful, willful ignorance. Most people in the book go on loving and serving him, so this is very hard to read. Justice is not done.

Another quality that makes the book painful is that the torments and injustices go on at great length, repetitively, for hundreds of pages. Really, you may get quite a sufficient taste of them from just the following sections concerning food and fish.

Sam Pollitt, the father, has been a fisheries inspector. Henny, his wife, hates him and fish. What she loves is tea. In an odd way, this massive book can be read as a kind of dialectic between the two: on one end stands what is sloppy, smelly, exploited, bloodily murdered, or suffocated by the likes of Sam and all that he self-righteously espouses; and on the other, what is genteel—but packs a wallop. Almost the first act in the book is Louisa's bringing tea to Henny (Louisa is the eldest of the six children and a virtual household slave). One of the last is Sam's boiling down a marlin for oil, followed by Henny's drinking a cup of tea poisoned by Louisa and meant for Sam. It is a measure of the misery of all concerned that Henny drinks the poison on purpose.

Louisa does much or most of the cooking, much or most of the child care, and also takes care of Henny. In return she is called "slummicker" and reviled as fat and disgusting by both parents. They mutually condemn Louie's extensive reading, her only escape. For the reader, Louie is the only hope of escape from the company of this nightmare claustrophobia-inducing couple.

For some reason, although Sam has an adequate salary, they have no money. Through his vanity and obliviousness, Sam manages to lose his job. Then the Pollitts are *really* poor. There may not be any love, but there's plenty of squalor.

You get to see the squalor most clearly when Louie has her adored teacher, Miss Aiden, to dinner. (Though God knows why Louie wants to, since she hates for anyone she likes to meet Sam, who always ruins everything and shames her.) Miss Aiden, at least, looks upon the works of Sam and sees that they are bad:

> She was shown the bathroom, and found herself in a shanty with wooden walls and a roughly cemented floor. One end of this was filled by a cement tub about five feet long by three deep; but the cement had a surface as rough as a coconut cake; Miss Aiden thought of submitting her soft, sleek, spoiled flesh to its gray rasping ridges and, thinking it impossible, looked about for a rubber sheet—they must use something to cover the cement when bathing. Everything was to match; home-made, rough and ready; instead of toilet paper, they used cut-up newspaper; there was no bathmat but a sodden crisscross of slats.

For the dinner,

> they came into a long, boarded room, with dirty window curtains, a battered dresser, homemade wall shelves, and a long, oak table with fat Victorian legs, on which hung a dirty, worn tablecloth covered with the old silver and stained knives. A thin glass vase, dirty napkins in rings, and one water glass with a Greek-key pattern engraved graced this cloth.

It occurs to Louie that "they had had no glasses for a long time."

Sam demands a salad after the stew Henny has served. Henny takes the younger daughter aside and says, "Tell your father that the snails ate the lettuce, and I had no money to buy trimmings!"

Miss Aiden is charmed by the handsome Sam nevertheless.

Sam relishes his unemployment and by the end of the book has shown no real sign of ending it. His occupation is to set the children upon outsize projects, order them around while mocking their efforts, and talk about how great the world would be if everyone were like him. The boiling of the marlin is the last of these projects shown, and the one dramatized in greatest detail. It takes place among the final crises of the novel: Sam's younger sister has just had an illegitimate baby, which has been sold by his older sister; and Henny has just returned from *her* sister—who keeps a fish shop. Henny was

hiding there because Sam received an anonymous note saying she'd been unfaithful (she had). The marlin, even before Sam gets to it, seems like any creature who's had too much to do with him:

> Its great eyes were sunken; it looked exhausted from its battle for life;
> there was a gaping wound in its deepest part. They attached it by a cord
> to a stake and immersed it in the creek, to keep it as fresh as possible till
> Sam came home.

This bootless project is all about stink and exhaustion.

> They were going to boil the fish through the night. There were basins
> alongside, on boards on top of the washtubs, into which the oil was to
> be ladled as it floated to the top; and all the washed bottles, with some
> gallon jars, stood along the wall of the washhouse . . .
>   In about twenty minutes, at about nine-forty-five in the evening, a
> strong smell of fish stew arose, which increased as the boiling went on.

Sam sets up a schedule of watches through the night, to "keep the fire,
skim the scum, stir the stew, and make a cup of tea for the watch to follow."
One boy asks Sam when Sam will watch. Sam answers that he is doing the
superintending, and "grinned wickedly" at them. These very little children
are practically perishing with exhaustion and from the stink through the long
night, in which there is a heavy storm. Sam crows that his cooking is

> worth something! What Sam-the-Bold cooks up ain't a angry stew like
> womenfolks. Sam-the-Bold cooks what air useful to man en horse en mo-
> torbike: the essential oil!

Sam habitually speaks in this kind of baby talk. As for the usefulness of his
cooking, it produces "nine large and five small bottles of unrefined marlin oil"
(not the predicted mere two gallons) and

> enough, with their kneading, manuring, trotting about, plastering, oiling,
> and dripping, to give Spa House [their derelict home] a scent of its own
> for many years to come.

While Sam has his children scattering the detritus for fertilizer, et cetera,
one of his twins, known as Little-Sam, throws up from the smell and exhaustion. Sam

took Little-Sam by the neck, drew him out of the washhouse, and, when he stood in the newly cemented yard outside the door, suddenly flung the liquid over him, drenching him. Little-Sam and the children were petrified with surprise. Sam did not even laugh but considered his son triumphantly. Not a tremor passed over the boy's face. He stood dripping with the juice, fish tatters on his head, one long shred of skin hanging down over one eye, making him look like the offspring of a mermaid and a beachcomber.

Then Sam takes the nap he would not let the children take.

This is very close to being the last straw for Louisa, though not for the other children, who mostly worship their father as they've been taught by him. Evie, the much younger girl, is flattered when Sam grotesquely tells her, "Little-Womey, soon you got to be my wife, I speck." (Earlier, he has been outraged that a very young girl, pregnant, attributed her condition to her father; he is outraged that the authorities believed her and deprived her father of her.)

It is a tribute to the long book that you finally hate Sam so much that you want Louie to kill him, and that you sympathize with Henny despite her callousness and perverseness. But the story is not told from anyone's point of view. Frankly, I'd rather just be allowed to enjoy Louisa's suffering as her partisan, as in a good Victorian novel—as in *A Little Princess*. We get exhausted, and mind the stink too.

Since I am not Sam, I am not going to try to force you to make something useful out of marlin, or insist that it is tasty. Instead, I offer another fatty fish of two syllables that ends in *n,* salmon. Sam was perfectly correct and before his time, as a conservationist of the 30s, to deplore overfishing and in particular the way the wealthy are catered to with sport fishing at the expense of great natural systems like the one at Chesapeake Bay, where the Pollitts' "Spa House" is. It is likely that new limits are going to have to be put on the catch of fish, in order to save them, which will make something like salmon even more expensive than it is now. The recipe that follows will still be a delicious way to cook it, however. It is the recipe of a very different kind of idealist (and father) from Sam—a former Weatherman, and a vegetarian and parent of two. "Sluggo" was his nom de guerre in the revolutionary Weather-underground of the 1960s.

Even though this uses sesame oil, the marinade is a perfect complement to big, fatty fish, and cuts their fatty taste. Unlike the classic combination of butter and lemon juice, the marinade also complements the fish-fat's bene-fits to the heart, being free of cholesterol.

Sluggo's Fish Fillet Marinade

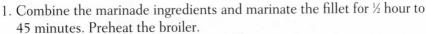

½ cup sesame oil
1 cup tamari or other soy sauce
½ cup fresh lime juice (about 3 limes)
¼ cup mirin*
2 tablespoons minced fresh garlic
2 tablespoons minced fresh ginger
Crushed red pepper flakes to taste
1 thick salmon fillet, up to 6–7 pounds (swordfish or
   tuna may be used instead)

1. Combine the marinade ingredients and marinate the fillet for ½ hour to 45 minutes. Preheat the broiler.
2. Place fish on broiling pan, skin side up. Spoon on tablespoon or so of mari-nade. Broil until skin is crisp (approximately 5 minutes). Turn, add a bit more marinade if you like, and broil till done (about 5 more minutes).

DINNER

Sluggo's Fish Fillet Marinade (recipe above)

Potato Slices Baked in Oil (recipe follows)

Mixed greens with garlic-mustard Vinaigrette**

---

*Mirin, a sweet sake for cooking, is available in Korean vegetable stores and other Asian markets, and in some supermarkets.
**Recipe in *The Sweet Dove Died*.

Potato Slices Baked in Oil

Potatoes cooked this way are like a slightly healthy cross between potato chips and french fries.

Slice as many potatoes as desired into rounds between ¼ and ½ inch thick.

Put enough oil in a baking pan to coat it generously. Lay the rounds in the oil, then turn them so that both sides are coated.

Bake at between 400° and 450°. When they begin to turn golden and puff, they may be turned over. When they puff and turn golden on the second side, they are done.

NOTE: An alternate method is to toss slices in a bowl with oil to coat and, if you wish, salt and/or herbs (such as herbes de Provence) or fresh herbs before spreading them on a baking sheet. For a less precise version, they can be spread thinly but not isolated like cookies, and simply scraped up and turned casually from time to time. They can also be cut in small chunks and roasted with the oil, or even, if they are small, cut just in half or kept whole. It is almost impossible to overcook such a dish—the potatoes are best when browned and semi-crisp. In this variation, you can also throw in whole unpeeled cloves of garlic or shallots, sliced mushrooms, quartered onions, etc.

SWANN'S WAY

by Marcel Proust

(1 9 1 3)

Translated by C.K. Scott Moncrieff and Terence Kilmartin (1981)

Asparagus nearly prevented me from reading *Remembrance of Things Past.* I tried reading the seven-volume book the first time in my mid-teens. I had been told it was about memory and time, but I found it dull to the point of stupefaction, mired in detail, its shape indiscernible. I tried again a few years later and was merely bored. Riffling ahead to see if more dramatic events were to emerge, I complained to my college roommate, "Asparagus! Two hundred pages and he's still going on about asparagus!" and slammed the book closed. So it remained until I was twenty-four. I finished *Swann's Way* at twenty-six and, considering that first volume as having been a good two years' work, had the second under my belt by twenty-seven. I read the final five volumes in two weeks and began the cycle again immediately. For a long time I read little else, and then realized I had better resume my own life. I now never read too much of Proust at any one time, for fear that this novel will take over my life again.

In the following passages from *Swann's Way,* asparagus is the pernicious fate of the hapless kitchen maid, whose life, as a result of it, can hardly be called her own.

> In the year in which we ate such quantities of asparagus, the kitchen-maid whose duty it was to prepare them was a poor sickly creature, some way "gone" in pregnancy when we arrived at Combray for Easter, and it was indeed surprising that Françoise allowed her to run so many errands and to do so much work, for she was beginning to find difficulty in bearing before her the mysterious basket, fuller and larger every day, whose splendid outline could be detected beneath the folds of her ample smock. This last recalled the cloaks in which Giotto shrouds some of his alle-

gorical figures, of which M. Swann had given me photographs. He it was who pointed out the resemblance, and when he inquired after the kitchen-maid he would say: "Well, how goes it with Giotto's Charity?"

These early portions of *Remembrance of Things Past* are a combination of low comedy intermixed with real tragedy. But since the narrator doesn't experience the tragedies, the scenes are presented as a series of amusing, beautiful, or terrible pictures. The narrator, young enough to be read to before bed (though one comes to feel he would happily have had the practice continue through about age sixty), stays, with his parents, at the house of his aunt Léonie Octave in the small rural town of Combray. Their cultivated but rather inadequately known fellow Parisian, Swann, has a place nearby, accessible by a path called, not so amazingly, Swann's Way. Swann has little to do in this section besides wander in being tactful and refined, but fanning around him a whiff of a more exciting, but hidden, world. It is Françoise, the fanatically faithful family retainer, and the hypochondriac Aunt Léonie—each of them rigid in her ideas about life, with their devotion to each other manifested in the form of unacknowledged war—who provide the comedy.

The first mention of asparagus comes from the mistress, who thinks that Françoise can get a better quality vegetable and mocks her as misguided.

> "Françoise, if you had come in five minutes ago, you would have seen Mme Imbert go past with some asparagus twice the size of mother Callot's: do try to find out from her cook where she got them. You know you've been putting asparagus in all your sauces this spring; you might be able to get some like those for our visitors."
>
> "I shouldn't be surprised if they came from the Curé's," Françoise would say.
>
> "I'm sure you wouldn't, my poor Françoise," my aunt would reply, shrugging her shoulders. "From the Curé's, indeed! You know quite well that he never grows anything but wretched little twigs of asparagus. I tell you these ones were as thick as my arm" . . .

We never quite know the resolution of that little dispute, but a few pages on, the aunt has found a new way to use asparagus in reproaching her house-keeper, who worries

> . . . "it's nearly ten o'clock and my fire not lighted yet, and I've still got to scrape my asparagus."
>
> "What, Françoise, more asparagus! It's a regular mania for asparagus you've got this year. You'll make our Parisians sick of it."

"No, no, Mme Octave, they like it well enough. They'll be coming back from church soon as hungry as hunters, and they won't turn their noses up at their asparagus, you'll see."

But little Marcel, uninvolved in the dramas being played out through the unlikely agency of a green vegetable, merely sees its beauty—though in Proust's case, beauty is never merely "mere":

> I would stop by the table, where the kitchen-maid had shelled them, to inspect the platoons of peas, drawn up in ranks and numbered, like little green marbles, ready for a game; but what most enraptured me were the asparagus, tinged with ultramarine and pink which shaded off from their heads, finely stippled in mauve and azure, through a series of imperceptible gradations to their white feet—still stained a little by the soil of their garden-bed—with an iridescence that was not of this world. I felt that these celestial hues indicated the presence of exquisite creatures who had been pleased to assume vegetable form and who, through the disguise of their firm, comestible flesh, allowed me to discern in this radiance of earliest dawn, these hinted rainbows, these blue evening shades, that precious quality which I should recognise again when, all night long after a dinner at which I had partaken of them, they played (lyrical and coarse in their jesting as the fairies in Shakespeare's *Dream*) at transforming my chamber pot into a vase of aromatic perfume.
>
> Poor Giotto's Charity, as Swann had named her, charged by Françoise with the task of preparing them for the table, would have them lying beside her in a basket, while she sat there with a mournful air as though all the sorrows of the world were heaped upon her; and the light crowns of azure which capped the asparagus shoots above their pink jackets were delicately outlined, star by star, as, in Giotto's fresco, are the flowers encircling the brow or patterning the basket of his Virtue at Padua . . .

Completely typical of Proust is this mingling of art, sex, and religion; also typical is the equally fluid exchange among human and botanic forms. And who but Proust would call that chemically altered urine "aromatic perfume"? Surely this is the most exquisite description of asparagus that can be written, an act of observation so intense as to constitute a drama in itself. When, as a too-youthful reader, I was waiting for something to "happen" in Proust, what I was failing to notice was that the descriptions constituted events.

There is, however, a human drama going on the whole time:

. . . Françoise had adopted, to minister to her unfaltering resolution to render the house uninhabitable to any other servant, a series of strategems so cunning and so pitiless that, many years later, we discovered that if we had been fed on asparagus day after day throughout that summer, it was because their smell gave the poor kitchen-maid who had to prepare them such violent attacks of asthma that she was finally obliged to leave my aunt's service.

Selecting Asparagus

M a n y people believe that asparagus like "wretched little twigs" is desirable, under the misconception that thin asparagus is younger. In fact, Aunt Léonie is quite right to demand asparagus as thick as her arm. The thickness of asparagus has nothing to do with maturity or age. A thick stalk of asparagus comes out of the ground that way, a thin one ditto. The only dimension that changes over time is length, and that changes *very fast*. A four-inch spear that you don't harvest in the morning may be more than a foot tall when you retrieve it from the garden at dinnertime. Ideally, you want to pick it (or have it picked) when it is about the length of a finger. You will never, however, get it this way unless you grow it yourself (or unless you have a very good friend who does—and I mean a *very* good friend, since almost no one grows so much that they can afford to give it away). Even at the farmers' market, yield is maximized by letting the stalks grow until they must either be harvested or allowed to go to their next stage, where they put out feathery fronds to collect nutrients for another year's growth and harvest. (You have to let that happen at some point: if you don't stop picking this perennial, you kill the goose that lays the golden eggs.) Also ideally, and also something you will never see in any market, the spears should be snapped off at ground level, without a knife. Whether cut, a foot long, or thin as twigs, raw harvested spears should be stored upright in an inch or two of water, like bouquets.

Marcel
Proust

Cooking Asparagus

In orthodox French cooking, the spears are cooked much the same way—upright, with their feet in water and their heads in the clouds. This seems pointless to me. Steam is at least as hot as boiling water (hotter, theoretically), so you are not cooking those tender little heads a bit less than the big tough feet. I lay them on a steamer, but I do put the thinner ones (which taste much more of stalk and much less of the vegetable's meat, but cook faster) on top of the fat ones—if I cook the two together at all.

Asparagus fresh from the garden barely needs any cooking. Cooks who have been told to leave their vegetables "crisp-tender" but don't have them fresh from the plant may opt for the darker flavor of non-crisp tenderness; otherwise, a stalk that has been allowed to sit around a supermarket drying out around the base will taste like wood. That's pretty much what that cellulose leached of its sugar is. Whether you like your asparagus soft or crisp, run it under cold water to stop the cooking when it gets to the point where you like it.

Like Françoise, you may want to "scrape" your asparagus before cooking, to remove the callous enveloping the cylinder. A vegetable peeler will do it, but rest the stalks against the counter or they will snap under its pressure. Hold them at the head end and scrape from the "shoulder" toward the base. You will, of course, have already cut off any trace of white at the base. Anyone who has disliked asparagus as "stringy" will discover that, peeled, it isn't.

Hollandaise is the classic accompaniment for asparagus, but it has a bad name these days. So long as you are not spooning it up like soup, however, it's probably not going to give you a heart attack right at the table. Vinaigrette is the more medically correct choice of the moment, and just plain lemon juice the most highly regarded of all by those whose goal it is to live like Aunt Léonie. With fresh, well-cooked asparagus, you cannot go wrong, and don't need to do anything to it at all. It's wonderful cut up in a soufflé, with oil and Parmesan in pasta, puréed in a quiche or pie, or added in inch or two lengths to a green salad. It is sublime in a creamy risotto like the one that follows. Otherwise, the best topping for it, if you are serving it as the vegetable side dish to people you really like, is lemon butter. While making lemon butter, you may wish that you had a kitchen maid. That is why it is important that the beneficiaries be dear to you—or you'll end up hating them.

Asparagus Risotto

The crucial element in any risotto is the broth. For a vegetable risotto, whether you use beef or chicken (or vegetable) broth, be sure that it is a very fully flavored broth, cooked down for intensity. Best of all is a good broth to which you have added the juices from roasted meat (or vegetable pan liquor). Canned broth really will make a poor risotto. Save leftover gravy when you have it to add to such broths.

However much rice you are using (of Arborio or other Italian-style brand), have on hand at least three times its amount in broth—i.e., for half a cup dry rice, have at least 1½ cups broth, etc. If you want a very vegetably risotto, use more asparagus; for a very full, rich, starchy dish, use a lower proportion. This can be either a side dish or an entrée. Don't worry about exactitude of amounts or timing; it is hard to go wrong with these ingredients, so long as you have enough broth and it is a tasty one.

> **Arborio or other Italian rice**
> **Olive oil**
> **Onion or shallot and/or garlic, chopped**
> **Strong, rich broth (3 times volume of rice used, or more)**
> **Asparagus, white part removed, cut on the diagonal into**
>   **1½–2-inch lengths**
> **Salt and/or fine white pepper (optional)**
> **Chopped fresh parsley**
> **Grated Parmesan cheese**

1. Bring the broth to a simmer, and maintain the simmer while preparing the risotto.
2. Coat the bottom of a deep, heavy, narrow pot with olive oil. Sauté chopped onion or shallots and/or garlic to desired doneness (transparent to brown).
3. Add rice and stir constantly over medium-high heat until opaque white.
4. With a teacup, measuring cup, or ladle, dip from the simmering broth about ½ cup and add it to rice. Stir. Keep stirring, gently, as the broth is absorbed. When the texture grows tacky, like rolled paint, add more broth and keep stirring. Continue to add broth and stir to tackiness for 20 minutes or more—until you have used most of the broth and your arm is falling off and you are sweating. Taste the rice. If it is beginning to taste cooked—just a little harder than *al dente*—throw in your asparagus with

the last dollop of added broth. It will cook while you stir. There should
be enough unabsorbed broth at the end so that the texture is creamy.
5. Add chopped parsley and Parmesan to taste.

NOTE: Risotto is not great if made in advance, and therefore not a great company dish if you like to talk to your guests—unless you are one of those genius cooks who can toss off jokes like sparks from a whetstone while actually
concentrating on the tasks at hand.

Lemon Butter

¾ pound very, very cold butter
½ cup freshly squeezed lemon juice
Salt and/or fine white pepper (optional)

1. Cut butter into tablespoon-size chunks and keep them refrigerated on a
   plate.
2. Cook lemon juice down to 1 or 2 tablespoons in medium saucepan. Reduce heat as far as possible. Add 1 chunk of butter, stirring with wire
   whisk until it is melted and creamy-looking. Keep whisking, adding each
   chunk as the previous one fully dissolves. The sauce will become thick
   and pale. You may want to add salt or some fine white pepper. This sauce
   can be kept warm indefinitely over water the same temperature as the
   sauce.

Makes about 1½ cups.

NOTE: The recipe can be extended by using more butter, as above. Allow
plenty of time for preparation.

DINNER

Asparagus Risotto (recipe above)

Chicken Livers in White Wine (recipe follows)

Sautéed mushrooms (oyster, porcini, cremini, in any combination)

Grapes of the Gods*

*Recipe in *Babette's Feast.*

Chicken Livers in White Wine

This may sound, and even be, elegant, but I first started making it as a college student living in a rooming house and using a cookbook with a name something like "Eating for a Dollar a Day." In those days you could—and well too.

   1 pound chicken livers, organic if possible (livers collect toxins)
   Butter or oil
   1–2 onions, chopped
   Basil, fresh or dried, to taste—probably quite a lot
   ⅓–⅔ cup dry white wine or chicken stock
   Salt and freshly ground black pepper, to taste

1. Wash and dry livers, removing filaments.
2. Coat a heavy skillet with butter or oil and sauté onions until golden. Raise heat and add livers and basil. Cook, stirring frequently, until livers are browned or cooked outside. Remove livers and onions, leaving liquid and scrapings in pan.
3. Pour in wine or stock and reduce by more than half, stirring in loosened scrapings.
4. Lower heat and return meat and onion to the pan. Allow barely to simmer until heated through (livers will be same color on the inside as on the outside). Add salt and pepper.

"STONE SOUP"

a n o n y m o u s

This is a folk tale in an extremely old mode that recounts the doings of a trickster or confidence man. It has myriad versions throughout Europe: a Swedish version in which the trickster is a tramp putting one over on an old woman, and at least one variation where the trickster is a young girl. A list of published versions can be found in *The Storyteller's Source Book,* on the reference shelf of most children's libraries. Variants include, as well as different tricksters, soup made with a nail and, in Russia, an ax.

The version most commonly encountered in America features three con men, foreign soldiers coming through a French village but unable to find food or lodging there. So they pretend to the peasants that they can provide their own food: they'll just make "stone soup." All they ask is a big cook pot, some water, and three round, smooth stones.

Stones the peasants always have too many of, and water seems to be the one thing they don't grudge. Fascinated at the prospect of making something out of nothing, the peasants stick around to watch how a stone soup is made. As the soldiers stir the unhopeful brew over the fire, they say it is going very nicely, but would be better if only they had some salt and pepper; the peasants bring some (spices were not as cheap or easy to come by centuries ago as they are now). Then the soldiers say the soup is fine but would be improved by the addition of carrots. A peasant, who has hidden her stock against the potentially marauding soldiers, retrieves some for the miraculous soup. The soldiers then express the wish for cabbages; for beef; for potatoes, barley, and milk. Each time they ask, they pretend the thought has just occurred to them. The peasants run to get the supplies, quite amazed at the soup "fit for a king" they are getting out of a stone. It seems like magic to them.

But then the peasants ask if the soup wouldn't be improved by the accompaniment of bread—and maybe some roast meat and cider while they're at it. The whole town ends up having a feast in the village square and thinking themselves lucky. They dance, gorge, and sing, and think stone soup is the best thing that's ever happened to them. The soldiers, in thanks, are given the three best beds in the village—at the priest's, the mayor's, the baker's, or the old woman's best featherbed. In the morning the peasants thank the tricksters, believing that their knowledge of how to make a soup from a stone will preserve them forever from hunger. So, as the story has come down to us, it's one big nudge in the ribs.

And a recipe. But it's not just a recipe for soup; it's a recipe for social welfare.

In the days when it arose, one can imagine soldiers embroidering on apocrypha about the credulous ignorance of peasants, especially foreign peasants. They needed to comfort themselves for hideous lives in which they had been forced into service (often from peasant villages) on threat of death, because why else serve in a job often without pay, equally often without food, in which you had to live out in the cold and walk across continents and exercise almost no free will, accumulate nothing, and quite likely lose an arm or eye if not be killed outright? At least soldiers have worldly wisdom, the story assures them.

It must have been a comfort to peasants too—at least they were not pillaged, killed, and raped, common enough means of coming by provisions for an army, even if they were portrayed as idiots. It might be safer to appear as idiots to hungry, armed, brutalized men.

In any case, the only trick here is not really played *on* anyone. Each gives according to his means to each according to their need, and what would be an intolerable burden for any individual householder—feeding and putting up the three hungry men—is lightly distributed across many, and becomes an entertainment valuable in itself. Would that our form of stone soup made for as much pleasure, as our tax contributions add up to buy surplus cheese for poor children on the one hand, or to plow under every fifth row of wheat on the other.

It may even be that a clean stone of advantageous composition can add nutritionally valuable minerals to a hearty soup.

Minestrone is not exactly what the soldiers and peasants made, but it has some shared ingredients. And if, on the principle of the soldiers, you say, "If only we had a little Parmesan," instead of milk, or ask for beans or macaroni instead of barley, you end up with minestrone. What minestrone has in common with stone soup is its ad hoc nature. It can be made just according to the recipe—or with almost any other set of vegetables and any good stock. If you start with dried beans, they are like pebbles if not actual stones.

Minestrone

This is ideal served with a crusty, chewy Italian whole wheat loaf and a soft Italian butter (Zito's bread and Sicura butter, if you're in New York City).

1–4 cloves garlic, chopped
1–3 onions, sliced
½ cup olive oil
1 cup (or more) chopped carrots or other root vegetable
2 cups (or more) chopped zucchini or summer squash
2–4 cups chopped potato
1 cup cut-up snap beans
3 cups sliced or shredded kale or cabbage
6 cups broth
Up to ⅓ pound Parmesan cheese—crust if possible, or
    cut into chunks
1 28-ounce can undrained crushed Italian tomatoes
1½ cups cooked white beans, *or* 1 cup uncooked dried pasta
    (shells, elbows, orzo, etc.)
Salt and freshly ground black pepper
Grated Parmesan cheese

1. Brown garlic and onions in oil. Add carrots, zucchini, potatoes, green beans, and kale, and sauté until they soften.
2. Add broth, Parmesan crust or chunks, and tomatoes. Cook over medium-low heat (at a lively simmer) about 3 hours.
3. Add white beans or pasta and cook until beans are heated through or pasta is *al dente*. Remove cooked Parmesan. Taste for seasoning; add salt and pepper if desired. Serve sprinkled with grated Parmesan.

Serves 6.

NOTE: To thicken, if desired: sieve out and purée a few spoonfuls of vegetables; stir the purée into the soup. Or, whisk in mashed potatoes or additional puréed beans.

LUNCH

Minestrone with grated Parmesan cheese (recipe above)

Italian bread

Soft butter

GOOD BEHAVIOUR

by Molly Keane

(1 9 8 1)

This is one of those British-style novels that begins with the end and goes backward, so that you only understand the full significance of the opening scene when you have read the rest.

In the opening scene, a daughter kills her mother by feeding her rabbit.

"Mummie" hates rabbit. She's also hated her daughter, Aroon St. Charles, all Aroon's life—and rabbit was sometimes Mrs. St. Charles's way of expressing it:

> When we were children [Aroon narrates] the food in the nursery was quite poisonously disgusting. None of the fruit juice and vitamins of today for us—oranges only at Christmastime and porridge every morning, variable porridge slung together by the kitchen maid, followed by white bread and butter and Golden Syrup. Boiled eggs were for Sundays and sausages for birthdays. I don't think Mummie gave us a thought— she left the ordering of nursery meals to the cook, who sent up whatever came easiest, mostly rabbit stews and custard puddings riddled with holes.

Aroon's powerlessness only increases with adulthood, as she grows into an ungainly young woman who can't do any of what matters to her class— ride bravely, repress all unseemly feelings, attract the right young men. So that when the stately Irish family can no longer pay its bills, and Aroon's father is incapacitated by a stroke, her mother proposes economizing thus:

> "Perhaps if you were willing to eat just a little less, we wouldn't have this appalling bill; of course you happen to be a big girl." She might as well have said: You happen to have three legs. I went on talking to the dogs. "And all for red meat . . . What meat is not red? I ask myself."

"Rabbit," I told her.

"Rabbit? Then we might have rabbit more often. Not that I can eat rabbit."

"Neither will the maids."

"Why do we have so many maids? All eating their heads off. A little brown bread and butter is enough for me. Thin bread and butter. Perhaps you and the dogs could sometimes manage with rabbit? . . ."

We see through the cracked lens of Aroon's naive self-delusions the kind of casually cruel aristocratic lovelessness that breaks children. Aroon's adored brother Hubert becomes a covert homosexual and suicidal drunk. His secret lover, Richard, lamely attempts to force himself to make a proper engagement for appearance's—and inheritance's—sake. The uncracked side of the lens shows the cruelty Aroon unconsciously learns and commits in the name of good behavior—for instance, those well-made rabbit quenelles she inflicts on her eminently deserving mother.

Mrs. St. Charles is not the first in the family to be killed with kindness. Mr. St. Charles died in a not totally dissimilar way, at the hands of the family housekeeper, Rose, who is in love with him—whose hands also deliver hand-jobs under his invalid's bedcovers, along with the forbidden whiskey that kills him (but also keeps him happy).

(It is her cooking Mr. St. Charles loved Rose for, at first. Aroon remembers the woman in intimate converse with her father: "They were speaking of the Eagle range and its awful appetites, of gulls' eggs, and how long to cook them. There were pauses, dragging out the time of giving and taking orders for luncheon; their voices had another world beyond them.")

It is the father's death that frees Aroon, since, to her mother's shock and horror, he leaves everything to her and not to his wife.

On the way to this point, Aroon has deluded herself that her brother's lover was actually hers (because he once made himself come into her room at night, where he was so repelled by her body that he left as soon as he could, having barely touched her). The bond among the brother and sister and his lover was the governess who at different times served them, Mrs. Brock. Hubert and Aroon grew up on tales of life in the house of her previous charge:

> . . . we could nearly taste the delicious little suppers . . . carried up to the schoolroom. Although these suppers had the Hunker-Munker *Two Bad Mice* quality of false dolls'-house food, the breathing life in her telling held us avid as a good rancid gossip about money or love might hold us in later life.

(They were indeed tinily doll-like suppers—hot soup and "a wing of chicken under a silver lid." A *wing*.)

Mrs. Brock, like Rose and all women, also adored Mr. St. Charles, who rewarded her servile devotion with

Exquisite, expensive chocolates. *"The* best," Mrs. Brock intoned happily. "Charbonnel AND Walker." Liqueur and coffee creams, powdered truffles, crystallized rose-leaves, crystallized violets, and a fresh mirror-smooth gleam on the row upon row and layer after layer that filled the big box, each chocolate as beautiful as a chocolate could be.

Mrs. St. Charles decides that the poor old governess is a "bad influence" and has her fired. Bereft, Mrs. Brock drowns herself. The children, for whom Mrs. Brock was the only warm spot in chilly childhoods, are embarrassed by her memory in later life—loving kindness, in their circles, *is* a bad influence— and treat even her death as a joke.

In this vicious upper-class world where cruelty so often goes under the name of "good behavior," it is no wonder that Aroon can convince herself of her own good deeds. Here are the events of that murderous opening scene:

"I wonder are you wise, Miss Aroon, to give her the rabbit?"

"And why not?" I can use the tone of voice which keeps people in their places and usually silences any interference from Rose. Not this time.

"Rabbit sickens her . . ."

"I've often known her to enjoy rabbit . . ."

"She never liked rabbit."

"Especially when she thought it was chicken."

"You couldn't deceive her, Miss Aroon." She picked up the tray. I snatched it back . . .

Aroon carries it up to her by this time invalid mother.

"Luncheon," I said cheerfully, the tray I carried making a lively rattle . . .

"I don't feel very hungry," she said. A silly remark. I know she always pretends she can't eat and when I go out makes Rose do her fried eggs and buttered toast and all the things the doctor says she mustn't touch.

"Smell that," I said, and lifted the cover off my perfect quenelles . . .

"Now then," I said—one must be firm—"a delicious chicken mousse."

"Rabbit, I bet," she said.

I was still patient: "Just try a forkful."

"Myxomatosis," she said. "Remember that?—I can't."

I held on to my patience. "It was far too young to have myxomatosis. Come on now, Mummie—" I tried to keep the firm note out of my voice—"just one."

She lifted the small silver fork (our crest, a fox rampant, almost handled and washed away by use) as though she were heaving up a load of stinking fish: "The smell—I'm—" She gave a trembling, tearing cry, vomited dreadfully, and fell back into the nest of pretty pillows.

I felt more than annoyed for a moment. Then I looked at her and I was frightened. I leaned across the bed and rang her bell. Then I shouted and called down to Rose in the kitchen. She came up fast, although her feet and her shoes never seem to work together now; even then I noticed it. But of course I notice everything.

"She was sick," I said.

"She couldn't take the rabbit?"

Rabbit again. "It was a mousse," I screamed at the old fool, "a cream mousse. It was perfect. I made it so I ought to know. It was RIGHT. She was enjoying it."

Rose was stooping over Mummie. "Miss Aroon, she's gone."

Thus, death by bunny. But then, this was the mother who said, complaining of the doctor's bills,

"He charged ten pounds when you were born. It was quite a ridiculous price." She looked through me, and back into the past. "Nothing's worth it," she said.

Though the book is written as a comedy, it is a grim one. It seems to concede this, albeit in Aroon's untrustworthy voice, when she writes at last, "I know I'm big, but I'm a girl, I suppose, not a joke."

N a t u r a l l y , after this you need a recipe for rabbit. The following stew may also, however, be made with chicken or veal. It has never, in my experience, made anyone sick—in fact, it's a great favorite. Because it is made with cider, it is set off well by a salad of tart greens and tomatoes with purple onion, or by spinach or braised endive, and served with boiled red potatoes or noodles. The sauce is so good that you may want to double the cooking liquid.

Rabbit Stew

2 tablespoons flour
½ teaspoon salt
1 grind black pepper
1 medium rabbit, cut into parts, *or* 2½ pounds chicken, cut into
    parts, *or* 1 pound veal, cut into stewing chunks
½ pound bacon, cut into 1-inch lengths
2 cloves garlic, chopped
1 large onion, chopped
3 stalks celery, leaves included, cut into 1-inch lengths
2 carrots, sliced
Cooking oil
1 cup hard cider (see Note)
2 tablespoons chopped fresh parsley
2 sprigs fresh thyme, chopped, or ½ teaspoon dried
2 fresh sage leaves, chopped, or a pinch dried

1. Mix flour, salt, and pepper and dredge meat in it.
2. Cook bacon. Remove the cooked bacon from pan, reserving fat, and
   sauté garlic and onion in the fat. Add carrots and celery and cook until
   wilted. Remove vegetables and reserve.
3. Add oil to pot if necessary, and brown dredged meat. Remove meat and
   deglaze pan with ¼ cup cider.
4. Return all ingredients to pot, adding the rest of the cider and the herbs.
   Cover and cook at low simmer for 1 hour.

Serves 4.

NOTE: If you do not have hard cider on hand, bottled alcoholic cider such as
the French brand "Pour Pommes" can be bought at liquor stores. "Wood-
pecker" English cider is sold like beer, if you can find it. Or you can try adding
⅛ to ¼ cup cider vinegar to ⅞ cup fresh cider.

DINNER

Rabbit Stew (recipe above)

Egg noodles or boiled new potatoes

*Salad of endive, tomato, and arugula or watercress, with slivers of
purple onion and Vinaigrette**

Gingerbread (recipe below)

*Recipe in *The Sweet Dove Died.*

Gingerbread

¼ pound sweet butter
½ cup brown sugar
½ cup molasses
2 eggs
1½ cups flour
½ teaspoon baking soda
1 tablespoon powdered ginger (or to taste)
1 teaspoon cinnamon
¼ teaspoon ground cloves
¼ teaspoon ground allspice
½ cup buttermilk
2 teaspoons vanilla extract
Confectioners' sugar

Preheat oven to 350°.

1. Cream butter and sugar together in a bowl large enough to hold all the ingredients. Add molasses. Beat in eggs.
2. Sift dry ingredients together. Combine the buttermilk and vanilla. Fold dry ingredients into the wet mixture in batches just until blended, alternating with buttermilk/vanilla mixture. Turn the batter into a well-greased 9 × 9 × 2 inch baking pan.
3. Bake between 20 and 30 minutes, until it has risen in the middle and tests done with a toothpick or skewer. Turn out onto a plate, then turn over onto a serving plate or wire rack to return to right side up for cooling. When cool, sprinkle with confectioners' sugar. If you want to be fancy, try the doily trick: place a large paper doily over the gingerbread and sprinkle the sugar through it, removing the doily without spilling the excess sugar. It makes snowflake patterns.

TIME ITSELF

THE MAGIC MOUNTAIN

by Thomas Mann

(1 9 2 4)

translated by H. T. Lowe-Porter

They had sat down at the raised table in the window, the pleasantest spot in the room, facing each other against the cream-colored hangings, their faces lighted by the red-shaded table-lamp. Hans Castorp clasped his freshly washed hands and rubbed them together in agreeable anticipation—a habit of his when he sat down to table, perhaps because his ancestors had said grace before meat. They were served by a friendly maid in black frock and white apron. She had a pleasant, throaty voice, and her broad face was indisputably healthy-colored. To his great amusement, Hans Castorp learned that the waitresses here were called "dining-room girls." They ordered a bottle of Gruaud Larose, and Hans Castorp sent it back to have it warmed. The food was excellent: asparagus soup, stuffed tomatoes, a roast with vegetables, an exceedingly well-prepared sweet, cheese, and fruit. Hans Castorp ate heartily, though his appetite did not turn out quite so stout as he had thought. But he always ate a good deal, out of pure self-respect, even when he was not hungry.

This is the first meal Hans Castorp has on the magic mountain, where he arrives for a three-week visit to his cousin, and stays seven years. The "magic mountain" is a sanatorium in the Alps, around 1909 in this early scene—a time when the major treatment for tuberculosis was rest and an enormous amount of food, almost as a homeopathic cure: fighting consumption by consuming. Hans's cousin, Joachim, is in treatment, though if food alone were the cure, he would hardly have needed to leave the opulence of their family home, where the orphaned Hans has grown up with his grandfather and uncles.

The housekeeping, for many years, had been the care of an Altona goldsmith's daughter, named Schalleen, who wore starched white ruffles at her plump, round wrists. Hers it was to see to it that the table, morning and evening, was richly laden with cold meats, with crabs and salmon, eel and smoked breast of goose, with tomato ketchup for the roast beef. She kept a watchful eye on the hired waiters when Consul Tienappel gave a gentlemen's dinner; and she it was who, so far as in her lay, took the place of a mother to little Hans Castorp.

It takes nearly a hundred pages for Hans to consume his first day's worth of meals at the Berghof sanitorium. Early breakfast is

pots of marmalade and honey, basins of rice and oatmeal porridge, dishes of cold meat and scrambled eggs; a plenitude of butter, a Gruyère cheese dropping moisture under a glass bell. A bowl of fresh and dried fruits stood in the centre of the table. A waitress in black and white asked Hans Castorp whether he would drink coffee, cocoa or tea. She was small as a child, with a long, oldish face—a dwarf, he realized with a start. He looked at his cousin, who only shrugged indifferently with brows and shoulders, as though to say: "Well, what of it?" So he adjusted himself as speedily as possible to the fact that he was being served by a dwarf, and put special consideration into his voice as he asked for tea. Then he began eating rice with cinnamon and sugar, his eyes roving over the table full of other inviting viands, and over the guests at the six remaining tables, Joachim's companions and fellow victims, who were all inwardly infected, and now sat there breakfasting.

This early breakfast is so huge that Hans greets breakfast proper with

"No . . . no, God help me, milk I never could abide, and least of all now! Is there perhaps some porter?" He applied himself to the dwarf and put his question with the gentlest courtesy, but alas, there was none. She promised to bring Kulmbacher beer, and did so. It was thick, dark, and foaming brownly; it made a capital substitute for the porter. Hans Castorp drank it thirstily from a half-litre glass, and ate some cold meat and toast. Again there was oatmeal porridge and much butter and fruit. He let his eyes dwell upon them, incapable of more. And he looked at the guests as well; the groups began to break up for him, and individuals to stand out.

Lunch teaches him a little more about the place:

The meal was as faultlessly prepared as it was abundant. Counting
the hearty soup, it consisted of no less than six courses. After the fish
followed an excellent meat dish, with garnishings, then a separate vegetable course, then roast fowl, a pudding, not inferior to yesterday
evening's, and lastly cheese and fruit. Each dish was handed twice and
not in vain. At all seven tables they filled their plates and ate: they ate
like wolves; they displayed a voracity which would have been a pleasure
to see, had there not been something else about it, an effect almost un-
canny, not to say repulsive. It was not only the light-hearted who thus
laced into the food—those who chattered as they ate and threw pellets
of bread at each other. No, the same appetite was evinced by the silent,
gloomy ones as well, those who in the pauses between courses leaned
their heads on their hands and stared before them.

Then,

At tea all the various beverages were served which it is possible to
serve at that meal. Miss Robinson drank again her brew made of rose-
hips, the grand-niece spooned up her yogurt. There were milk, tea, coffee, chocolate, even *bouillon;* and on every hand the guests, newly arisen
from some two hours' repose after their heavy luncheon, were busily
spreading huge slices of raisin cake with butter.

And finally,

He dressed conscientiously for the evening meal, and, sitting in his
place between Miss Robinson and the schoolmistress, he ate: julienne
soup, baked and roast meats with suitable accompaniments, two pieces
of a tart made of macaroons, butter-cream, chocolate, jam and marzipan,
and lastly excellent cheese and pumpernickel. As before, he ordered a
bottle of Kulmbacher. But, by the time he had half emptied his tall glass,
he became clearly and unmistakably aware that bed was the best place
for him. His head roared, his eyelids were like lead, his heart went like
a set of kettledrums, and he began to torture himself with the suspicion
that pretty Marusja, who was bending over her plate covering her face
with the hand that wore the ruby ring, was laughing at *him*—though he
had taken enormous pains not to give occasion for laughter.

So the first "symptoms" are introduced—for Hans will summarily be di-
agnosed as having harbored TB. He is only too delighted to be asked to stay:

at last this orphaned "delicate child of life" (he is in his early twenties) feels he is a part of something.

Time passes slowly when he first arrives, then more and more quickly, until whole years disappear without his noticing. This is because of the un-varying routine of the Berghof, of which meals make so large a part: "motion from point to point is no motion more, where uniformity rules; and where motion is no more motion, time is no longer time. . . . there was no time up here to speak of, either long or short." Persephone refused to eat or to drink from the river Lethe, and could leave her place of entrapment after six months. Hans, eating those huge meals, forgets life in the "flatland" and is held fast.

Hans, however, though often described as dim, is ennobled by his stay in the enchanted realm, and becomes capable of insights like this central one that reflects exactly what has happened to him on the magic mountain—what makes it magic:

> "Hermetics—what a lovely word, Herr Naphta! I've always liked the word hermetic. It sounds like magicking, and has all sorts of vague and extended associations. You must excuse my speaking of such a thing, but it reminds me of the conserve jars that our housekeeper in Hamburg—Schalleen, we call her, without any Miss or Mrs.—keeps in her larder. She has rows of them on her shelves, air-tight glasses full of fruit and meat and all sorts of things. They stand there maybe a whole year—you open them as you need them and the contents are as fresh as on the day they were put up, you can eat them just as they are. To be sure, that isn't alchemy or purification, it is simple conserving, hence the word conserve. The magic part of it lies in the fact that the stuff that is conserved is with-drawn from the effects of time, it is hermetically sealed from time, time passes it by, it stands there on its shelf shut away from time. Well, that's enough about the conserve jars."

Time, it has been said, is the true hero of all novels. Thomas Mann is probably alone among great writers in making it with perfect explicitness the subject of this one.

W h a t Hans Castorp calls "conserves" is actually a conflation of a num-ber of processes—canning, conserve-making, and pickling—since "fruit and meat and all sorts of things" require different methods of preserving safely in jars. What they have in common is that they are "hermetically sealed from time." Practically any kind of food may be canned, but almost no one both-ers with this cumbersome technical process anymore: between commercial canning, which actually uses cans, and home freezing, which is much easier than canning, it is close to obsolete. For home canning you need equipment like a canner, which registers degrees of pressure, and an understanding of words like "petcock" (don't ask). Making conserves and pickles, on the other hand, requires nothing more than jars and cook pots, and is worth doing even if you are not preserving your own home-grown fruits and vegetables. In attractive glass jars with hand-written labels, conserves and pickles still make a special and useful old-fashioned gift.

to sterilize jars

Place jars on sides in pan of cold water to cover. Bring water to boil and boil 10 minutes. Treat jar covers the same way, either together with jars or separately. Let them remain in the heated water until you have the pickles or conserves ready to place inside them. Handle the jars with sterilized tongs.

Rubber seals should be boiled 2 minutes. Measuring cups, spoons, and any other utensils used in preparing the conserves or pickles should also be dipped in the boiling water.

filling and sealing

Fill the jars as soon as possible after sterilization so the jars will still be hot. Pour in the conserves or pickle brine while hot (though not boiling) and seal the jars right away. Tip jars to check seal. If they leak, check cover and rubber seal. If either is cracked, perforated, dented, or whatever, replace with a new one (sterilized).

cooling

After filling and sealing, set the jars aside to cool. Place jars upright far enough apart so they may cool easily but out of drafts so they will not crack. (It is sudden, steep changes in temperature that makes glass crack.) When jars are cold, test seal again by turning jars over in your hands. A metal lid should make a clear, ringing sound if tapped with a spoon, and be curved slightly inward.

If you are insecure, just because the process is slightly scary, about whether all is properly sealed and sterilized, you can keep the cooled jars in the refrigerator, after a week or so at room temperature. Be sure to tell anyone you give them to that they should refrigerate the jars. Always put the date on the label.

Pickled Green Tomatoes

If you have a garden or a friend with a garden, you know that when the first frost threatens, you usually have vines covered with green tomatoes. You can cut them down and hang them in a basement or put the fruits in brown paper bags (not on the windowsill) to ripen; you can also slice and bread the green fruit and fry it. But there is a way to keep this taste of summer indefinitely by preserving the fruits in brine. Some specialty stores and farmers' markets will sell you green tomatoes.

> 7–10 medium green tomatoes, or equivalent volume of small
> green tomatoes
> Mustard seed
> 3 cloves garlic
> Dill sprigs with blossoms
> 2 quarts water
> ¾ cup cider vinegar
> ½ cup non-iodized salt

1. Soak tomatoes overnight in cold water; drain, wash, and dry.
2. Place pinch of mustard seed and 1 clove garlic in each of three 1-quart sterilized jars. Add the whole tomatoes and dill blossoms alternately until jars are filled. (The jars should still be very hot.)
3. Boil water, vinegar, and salt. Remove from heat to stop the boil. Pour the hot but not boiling liquid into the jars to cover tomatoes, and seal jars at once.

Makes 3 1-quart jars.

Cranberry Conserve

An ideal hostess gift for Thanksgiving.

> 1 quart (1 pound) cranberries, washed and stems removed
> 1½ cups water
> ¼ cup raisins, chopped

1 orange, juice and zest only
1 lemon, juice and zest only
1 apple, peeled, cored, and chopped
2½ cups sugar
1 cup broken walnuts

1. Simmer cranberries with half the water until they begin to peel open. Add remaining ingredients except walnuts and cook another 15 minutes, or until thickened.
2. Add walnuts and pour into hot, sterilized jars.

Makes about 2 quarts, or eight 8-ounce jars.

Pear Conserve

Excellent as garnish for duck, goose, turkey, or ham, or, for dessert, served with vanilla ice cream or gingerbread.

2 quarts (2 pounds) pears (4 good-size firm
    but ripe Boscs, or the equivalent)
⅓ pound sugar
Juice of 1 lemon
Juice of ½ orange

1. Halve, pare, and core the pears and slice them into thick semicircles. Place the slices in a bowl, sprinkle with the sugar, cover the bowl, and let stand overnight. The pears will give up juice to half-fill the bowl.
2. Drain pears, reserving juices. Simmer juices about 12 minutes, until syrupy.
3. Add pears and lemon and orange juice. Cover and cook over low heat about 1 hour. Syrup should be thick and somewhat transparent. Pour into hot sterilized jars and seal.

Makes about 1 quart, or four 8-ounce jars.

Rhubarb Conserve

3 cups half-inch pieces of rhubarb
3 cups sugar
3 oranges, juice and zest only
1 lemon, juice and zest only
½ pound almonds, coarsely chopped (optional)

1. Simmer all ingredients except nuts together for 30 minutes. Add almonds and cook another 5 minutes.
2. Pour into hot sterilized jars and seal.

Makes about 1 quart, or four 8-ounce jars.

DINNER

Roast duck with Cranberry Conserve (recipe above)

Fresh spinach sautéed in olive oil, with dash of nutmeg

Mix of brown and wild rice

Creamed Turnip Casserole (recipe follows)

Pear Conserve (recipe above) with vanilla ice cream and

crumbled amarétti

Turnip Casserole

Approximately 3 pounds white turnips, peeled
8 ounces softened cream cheese
¼ cup sugar or less, to taste
¼ pound sweet butter
Bread crumbs

Preheat oven to 350°.

1. Cook turnips in boiling water until just tender, then mash. (Should make about 6 cups.)
2. Add cream cheese, sugar, and butter and combine well, or process together in a food processor.
3. Turn into loaf pan or soufflé dish. Top with bread crumbs, and bake until hot and light brown.

Serves 6 to 8.

"BABETTE'S FEAST"

from ANECDOTES OF DESTINY

by Isak Dinesen

(1 9 5 8)

"*Babette's Feast*" is a fairy tale—in which art takes the place of magic.

The two beautiful and good sisters of this tale are the daughters of a revered religious leader of a small, Shaker-like puritan sect in Norway. In their youth the sisters were courted, respectively, by a dashing military man and a magnificent opera singer. The girls did not even consider what was offered— great love, on the one hand, and stardom as a singer on the other—though the one daughter liked the officer and the other loved singing. They chose instead to carry on their father's austere work with the tiny aging sect, so that after his death, living penuriously and abstemiously, their life is confined to the elderly and eventually bickering, feuding cluster.

One day in 1871, a Frenchwoman arrives on their doorstep, nearly dead from cold and privation, with a note from the opera singer asking that she be looked after, and saying that, in addition to possessing "resourcefulness, majesty and true stoicism . . . Babette can cook."

Like any mysterious, good-looking stranger in a fairy tale, Babette has special abilities: "She had appeared to be a beggar; she turned out to be a conqueror." Working for nothing, she soon has the household in better, more comfortable order than it has enjoyed perhaps ever, and for her bargaining prowess she is held in "awe" in the marketplace. Her soups and food-baskets have a "mysterious power to stimulate and strengthen" the poor and sick they are sent to. The sisters, suddenly and "miraculously" better off, feel uncomfortably that their somewhat incommunicative Babette may be a witch, or possibly a former incendiary in the Communard rebellion that forced her flight to Norway, and in which she lost her husband and son.

Babette is not allowed to cook French food: in France, "people ate frogs." She gives the sisters, as they ask, split cod and an ale-and-bread soup. The sisters come to rely on her so much that their great fear is of Babette's potentially winning the French lottery, in which she keeps an annually renewed ticket, and leaving them.

After twelve years, Babette wins the lottery.

The sisters, and the whole community, assume that Babette is leaving. However, after allowing the sisters to count and handle the enormous amount of money that has come to her, Babette asks a favor: to let her cook the dinner in celebration of their dead father's one hundredth birthday.

They really don't want to let her. It makes them nervous. But Babette, in all her salaryless years with them, has never asked for anything. They feel that they have to say yes. They are especially unhappy at consenting when Babette speaks of its being "a real French dinner," and even more so when a live tortoise arrives as part of the preparations. They decide, with their fellow believers, that nothing "set before them, be it even frogs or snails, should wring a word from their lips."

It's really too bad, because what is set before them turns out to be one of the best meals that has ever been prepared, or even thought of, anywhere—a fairy tale feast. It includes what the officer turned general, serendipitously present for the feast, calls "the finest Amontillado I ever tasted," followed by what he recognizes as "Blinis Demidoff." He is the only person worldly enough to appreciate what is served: "Veuve Cliquot 1860," real turtle soup (that tortoise), and a dish only the greatest chef in Paris had ever made—"a woman!"—called "Cailles en Sarcophage." (All we are told of these "quail in coffins" is that they are "incredibly recherché and palatable.") At the last, grapes, in December. The general recognizes this as the food that "no longer distinguishes between bodily and spiritual appetite or satiety."

All the feuds among the brethren and sistern cease on the spot. Even so, they don't acknowledge the food. They do perceive that they "had been given one hour of the millennium." Still, all the sisters can think of to tell Babette by way of thanks is "that it was a nice dinner." They tell her they will remember the evening when she has gone back to Paris.

But Babette is not going back to Paris. The kicker is that she has spent her entire winnings on the fabulous and elaborate meal. The sisters can't understand how so much could even be spent on a meal. Or why anyone would want to do it. In the course of this most revelatory conversation they have ever had with their servant, Babette discloses her past as the cook at the famous Paris restaurant that the general recalled. "Dear Babette," says one sister, "you ought not to have given away all you had for our sake."

"For your sake?" she replied. "No. For my own."

She rose from the chopping block and stood up before the two sisters.

"I am a great artist!" she said.

She waited a moment and then repeated: "I am a great artist, Mesdames."

Again for a long time there was deep silence in the kitchen.

Then Martine said: "So you will be poor now all your life, Babette?"

"Poor?" said Babette. She smiled as if to herself. "No, I shall never be poor. I told you that I am a great artist. A great artist, Mesdames, is never poor. We have something, Mesdames, of which other people know nothing."

The sisters embrace Babette and tell her that when she gets to cook in Paradise she will "be the great artist that God" meant her to be: "Ah, how you will enchant the angels!"

The story is the converse of Peretz's "Bontshe," for here it is the solitary self-dependent one who provides and who, in heaven, instead of receiving like a beggar, will bring gifts. It is fitting that this should be the case where food is art: in the realm of art, regardless of the medium—words, paint, sound, movement—the artist does not distinguish "between bodily and spiritual appetite," or rather, they become one and the same. The physical medium becomes, while most sensuous and most itself, the means of metaphor: transcendent, and the mind-stuff of the beings who take it in. The artist does not have to wait for heaven or the millennium, for she creates them, in discrete portions, minute by minute, in her work. Great art stops time. (In life, where the millennium awaits, the artist may, like Babette, also have to become a revolutionary.) This is to cross the circle from Persephone, a god's victim. If Persephone could have cooked like Babette, she probably could have conjured Pluto into releasing her, and would not have had to spend six months starving and half the rest of her life in hell.

Isak Dinesen, or rather Karen Blixen, the real person behind the pen name, is said to have lived on nothing but oysters, grapes, and champagne for the last years of her life. Pictures of her show something like an animated cadaver. Maybe it was thinking of the foods she no longer allowed herself that in part generated this tale (or maybe she still ate quail and soup and all the rest in addition to Veuve Cliquot and grapes). Either way, this grape dessert seems appropriate.

Green and Purple Grapes of the Gods

1 pound seedless green grapes
1 pound purple grapes
3 tablespoons sugar
Zest of 1 lemon, grated
Juice of 3 oranges

1. Wash grapes. To remove seeds from purple grapes, cut the grapes in half, letting them rotate under the knife around the seeds. Pull halves apart. Pull seeds out. Detach all stems.
2. Mix sugar, lemon zest, and orange juice. Pour over grapes, and combine. Liquid should just cover grapes.
3. Refrigerate until ready to serve. Do not make more than 10 hours before serving, as grapes may ferment.

Serves 6.

NOTE: Though it was enough for Babette, in the nineteenth-century Norway winter, to serve grapes at all, spoiled moderns may want simple cookies or a plain cake by way of accompaniment to this tangy, sweet concoction.

Since most of us don't inhabit fairy tales, it is unlikely we can usher in an interval of the millennium by what we cook. For me, those meals that have come closest to such a feeling have not necessarily been the most elaborate—sometimes it is just a serendipitous combination of leftovers and what's in the house that turns into an ambrosial but unrepeatable dinner. Sometimes it's the company and circumstances—a June picnic in a field of blooming wild flowers with close friends.

Besides, between the meal's cost and the unavailability of turtles, duplicating Babette's feast is pretty much out of the question. (Even *mock* turtle soup would be a bit of a nightmare for the home cook: it is made with a whole calf's head, boned, and requires a food press to squash the head.) Nor have I been able to find out exactly what Blinis Demidoff are (if they exist outside Dinesen's imagination). There are any number of ways to make the little pancakes that are blini, but they are all served with caviar or smoked fish and the usual condiments. I drew the same blank in researching quail in their coffins. It was in no book of nineteenth-century French cuisine I found, or in contemporary cookbooks either—naturally: it's Babette's own invention. The movie of *Babette's Feast* interpreted the recipe as whole roast quail in pastry shells, with their little limp heads drooping over the edges, beaks dangling. A more conventional recipe is roast quail (sans heads) in nests made of potato straws: very cute, and with happier connotations than graves. But I am not Babette, and neither are you, and cooking *that* complicated is my idea of hell, not heaven. The traditional combination of quail, potatoes, and grapes seems most delicious to me. The inclusion of grapes, however, knocks out Grapes of the Gods as a dessert for this particular feast.

Part of what makes Babette's food sound so celestial is the very lack of description—the food is more spirit than substance. That leaves it up to us to flesh out. So here is the menu I propose for our earthly feast. It may even be as good as Babette's. The billi bi alone—cream of mussel soup—is heavenly, if not millennial.

FEAST

Buckwheat Blini (recipe follows) with smoked fish or caviar

Billi Bi (recipe follows)

Quail with Potatoes and Grapes (recipe follows)

Tirami Su (recipe follows)

Because this meal is so wickedly unbalanced, you may wish to add a salad or other green vegetable.

Buckwheat Blini

Nothing can quite prepare you for the sensation of the hot, crisp pancake and cold juicy roe popping against your tongue.

  1 cup milk
  ½ package yeast
  4 eggs, separated
  ½ teaspoon salt
  1 teaspoon sugar
  3 tablespoons butter, melted
1½ cups sifted buckwheat flour

1. Scald milk. Cool to body temperature or just above. Stir in yeast.
2. Beat egg yolks to mayonnaise consistency. Add remaining ingredients except egg whites. Blend.
3. Set bowl in warmish place, cover with cloth, and let dough rise until doubled in bulk, around 1¼ hours.
4. Beat egg whites till stiff. Fold into batter (which will sink). Allow second rising, 30 to 40 minutes.
5. Heat griddle over low to medium heat, using just enough butter to coat. Drop batter by tablespoonfuls onto griddle and cook as you would pancakes. Blini should be edged with brown, and golden-flecked. Add butter to pan as needed, keeping it to the thinnest film.

NOTE: Serve with caviar in a bowl set in ice, or with thin slices of Norwegian or Scottish smoked salmon, plus: a bowl of sour cream, a bowl of chopped hard-boiled egg, and a bowl of chopped onion, all to scatter over blini as desired. Lemon wedges may also be set out.

Makes approximately 36 blini; serves between 6 and 10 for appetizers.

Billi Bi

2 shallots, chopped
2 small onions, quartered
2 pounds mussels, cleaned and scrubbed
2 sprigs parsley
Salt and freshly ground black pepper
Pinch of cayenne pepper
1 cup dry white wine
2 tablespoons butter
1 small bay leaf
½ teaspoon dried thyme, or several sprigs fresh
2 cups heavy cream
1 egg yolk, beaten slightly

1. Sauté shallots and onions lightly in the butter, then add all other ingredients except cream and egg. Cover pot and allow mixture to simmer at medium heat for 5 to 10 minutes, just until mussels open. (Any mussels that do not open were dead before cooking and should be thrown out.)
2. Set mussels aside. (They may be used as garnish for the soup, but they ruin the creamy texture. Save them for pasta sauce, or feed them to the cat.) Line a strainer with two layers of cheesecloth and strain soup mixture into pot.
3. Bring to boil and add cream. Let it heat to the point where it bubbles, and cook briefly. Remove a cup or so from heat and stir or whisk egg yolk into it, letting the mixture thicken without making strips of hard-boiled yolk. Remove soup pot from heat and add egg mixture, stirring. Cook over low heat just long enough to thicken a little, stirring: boiling at this point can ruin the soup. Serve hot or chilled.

Serves 2 to 4.

Quail with Potatoes and Grapes

This classic high-French recipe is, mercifully, pretty simple and fast—you pan-roast some cut-up potatoes, then torture some miniature poultry, boil up the liquids, and have something delicately rich with edges both of sweetness and tartness.

Quail are so tiny, it hurts to see their babylike bodies. In this recipe, they are cooked by briefly browning, roasting, singeing, and simmering. I don't see the need for trussing, but that is the classical way. Each person gets two, like Gulliver in Lilliput.

This is a delicious way to cook potatoes—home-fries that taste roasted—but they can stick despite the occasional shake. A flat-sided wooden spoon can gently loosen and toss them, but do it quickly; it's best to keep the lid closed. (A glass-topped pot can tell you if your potato cubes are moving or stuck.) It takes a little time, twenty minutes or more, for the potatoes to be tender but firm, with crisp faces.

  8 tablespoons sweet butter or as needed
  4 medium potatoes, peeled, cut in ½-inch cubes, rinsed, and
      patted dry
Kosher salt and freshly ground black pepper
  8 quail
1½–2 cups grapes, seedless or seeds removed
  4 tablespoons cognac
  ½ cup chicken stock
  ¼ cup dry white wine

Preheat oven to 425°.

1. Melt a third of the butter (about 2½ tablespoons). Add potato cubes, salt them, turn to coat, and cover pan. Cook over low heat for 20 minutes or more, shaking pot occasionally to turn cubes, until potatoes are soft and lightly browned. Remove from heat and keep warm.
2. Rinse and dry quail. Salt and pepper skin and cavities. Truss, if desired.
3. Melt half the remaining butter and brown quail, turning. Place pan in hot oven 8 minutes. Add the grapes and roast another 2 minutes.
4. Place pan on stove and add cognac. Light the liquid with a match and allow flame to burn itself out. Add the stock and wine and cover, bringing liquid nearly to the boil for 2 minutes.
5. Untruss birds and remove to heated platter or serving plates. Add remaining butter to sauce and boil it, stirring, for 2 minutes at high heat. Pour sauce with grapes over quail and surround with potatoes.

Serves 4.

Tirami Su

Tirami su isn't French and may not go as far back as the nineteenth century, but the mascarpone cheese with which this is made is one of the most delicious substances extant. In pizzerias in Italy, you can get a plain mascarpone dessert served like soft ice cream, in a swirled peak. In some restaurants you can sometimes get mascarpone ravioli. They say, "See Rome and die." No. Taste mascarpone. After that, not too much matters. For a little while, anyway.

 5 egg yolks
¼ cup sugar
1¼ cups mascarpone
 1 cup heavy cream
6–9 double ladyfingers
¾ cup just-brewed espresso
¼ cup powdered chocolate

1. Beat yolks with sugar until light and thick. Beat mascarpone in thoroughly.
2. Whip cream and fold cheese mixture into it.
3. Dip ladyfingers into the espresso. Place side by side in a dish roughly 9½ × 13½ inches with sides at least 2 inches high. (A flat-bottomed bowl can also be used.) Unload cream mixture over ladyfingers and smooth evenly. Using a small strainer, sifter, or shaker, dust surface with chocolate. Refrigerate until ready to serve.

Serves 6 to 10.

For a lighter, late summer or early autumn dessert, you can core whole ripe pears and stuff them with mascarpone. To serve, the pears should be laid on their sides and sliced through the core, yielding circlets of pear with cheese centers. Garnish with nuts and a sprinkling of sugar.

Permissions

Grateful acknowledgment is made to the following authors, publishers, and copyright holders for permission to quote from the works indicated below:

James M Cain's *Serenade*, © 1937, 1965 by James M. Cain. Reprinted by permission of Alfred A. Knopf, Inc.

Colette's "Julie de Carneilhan," translated by Patrick Leigh Fermor. Copyright © 1952, 1980 by Farrar, Straus & Giroux, Inc. Reprinted by permission of Farrar, Straus & Giroux, Inc.

Roald Dahl's "Lamb to the Slaughter" from *Tales of the Unexpected*, © 1990 Vintage. Reprinted by permission of the author and the Watkins/Loomis Agency.

Isak Dinesen's *Anecdotes of Destiny*, © 1958 by Isak Dinesen. Reprinted by permission of Random House, Inc., and of the Rungstedlund Foundation.

Stella Gibbons's *Cold Comfort Farm*, © Stella Gibbons 1932. Reproduced by permission of Curtis Brown, London.

Molly Keane's *Good Behaviour*, © 1981 by Molly Keane. Reprinted by permission of Alfred A. Knopf, Inc.

Doris Lessing's *The Diaries of Jane Somers: The Diary of a Good Neighbor and I*, © 1983 by Doris Lessing. Reprinted by permission of Alfred A. Knopf, Inc., and reprinted by kind permission of Jonathan Clowes Ltd., London, on behalf of Doris Lessing.

Thomas Mann's *The Magic Mountain*, translated by H.T. Lowe-Porter, © 1927, 1955 by Thomas Mann. Reprinted by permission of the publisher. Reprinted also by permission of Martin Secker & Warburg.

Alice Munro's *The Beggar Maid*, © 1977, 1978 by Alice Munro. Reprinted by permission of Alfred A. Knopf, Inc. Under the title *Who Do You Think You Are?*, © 1978 by Alice Munro, reprinted by permission of Macmillan Canada.

Marcel Proust's *Remembrance of Things Past*, translated by C.K. Scott-Moncrieff and T. Kilmartin. Translation © 1981 by Random House and Chatto and Windus. Reprinted by permission of Random House, Inc.

Barbara Pym's *The Sweet Dove Died* © 1978 by Barbara Pym. Used by permission of Dutton Signet, a division of Penguin Books USA Inc. and by Macmillan General Books.

Christina Stead's *The Man Who Loved Children*, © 1940, 1968 by Christina Stead. Reprinted by arrangement with the Estate of Christina Stead, c/o Joan Daves Agency as agent for the proprietor.

GENERAL INDEX

RECIPE INDEX